SONYA SHANNON

TRANSFORMATION ORACLE

REDFeather

MIND | BODY | SPIRIT

An Imprint of Schiffer Publishing, Ltd.

Published by Red Feather Mind, Body, Spirit
An imprint of Schiffer Publishing, Ltd.
4880 Lower Valley Road
Atglen, PA 19310
Phone: (610) 593-1777; Fax: (610) 593-2002
E-mail: Info@schifferbooks.com
Web: www.redfeatherpub.com

For our complete selection of fine books on this and related subjects, please visit our website at www.schifferbooks.com. You may also write for a free catalog.

Schiffer Publishing's titles are available at special discounts for bulk purchases for sales promotions or premiums. Special editions, including personalized covers, corporate imprints, and excerpts, can be created in large quantities for special needs. For more information, contact the publisher.

We are always looking for people to write books on new and related subjects. If you have an idea for a book, please contact us at proposals@ schifferbooks.com.

CONTENTS

ABOUT TRANSFORMATION ORACLE

I created the *Transformation Oracle* to guide you on your spiritual journey. Oracles are a great way to get an "x-ray view" into a situation! The 44 images in the oracle are inspired by Divine Wisdom and are intended for your growth. I crafted each card from prayer and unconditional love in a meditative state. The visual symbols and their meanings hold deep mysteries and insights about how the Universe works, and the forces that touch your life. Because this is a channeled deck, it tends to be highly accurate—especially if you connect first with Spirit. Special blessings for you and your loved ones infuse every color, shape, and word!

The *Transformation Oracle* was channeled to serve our spiritual growth during the time of the Planetary Shift. This cosmic event heralds the start of the Aquarian Age, a time when old, Piscean Age structures are crumbling. The Piscean time was defined by pyramidical social structures, with a king or emperor on top and widening layers of lesser power below. As that Age deteriorates, the new Aquarian structures emerge, defined by the interconnectivity and personal empowerment of the internet. This lattice structure gives us each a voice, plus unlimited access to the world's knowledge bases and records. The Planetary Shift is a time of great turbulence and potential darkness politically, environmentally, and socially. If you found your way to this oracle, chances are you are a Light Worker, one who has been tested by the fires of great difficulties in life in order that the Divine Light may shine more clearly through you. The *Transformation Oracle* is a tool for bringing even more Light into your life. Whether you read for yourself or others, the cards and their meanings are guided by the Divine to bring about healing, spiritual growth, and positive changes.

This deck is grounded in the four elements: **Earth**, **Air**, **Fire**, and **Water**. Some divination systems, like the I-Ching, use five elements, with the fifth element being metal or ether. The Spirit Guides for this oracle specifically instructed that it needs only four elements. Everyone knows these four elements as Body (Earth), Heart (Water), Mind (Air), and Spirit (Fire). As human beings, we're already experts in them! Because the Planetary Shift is a time of complexity and seemingly endless learning curves, the *Transformation Oracle* is intended to help you immediately and intuitively, calling on the wealth of your existing life experience and intersecting with knowledge you have already acquired.

A unique aspect of this oracle is that it came through visually first. The images appeared in 44 perfect visions that were eidetically translated into artware—an art form that uses the complex Aquarian technologies of photography, special visual effects, and mathematical transformations. Where most oracle, angel, or Tarot decks are first written by an author who then seeks illustrations, this guidebook was written after the artware was created. Much is in the artware that cannot be described, so please use your gifts to read the visuals and trust what you see at least to the degree that you trust the words on these pages.

THE FOUR ELEMENTS

Since ancient times, the four elements were considered the foundation of our Universe. All things are made of Earth, Air, Fire, and Water. As we transform, these elements recombine in specific ways to bring about change. ▽ **Earth** is *grounding and centering.* It represents the physical realm: our body, living space, and finances. Earth is our home and the center of being. Its qualities are productivity, fertility, and abundance. If you draw an Earth card, the message concerns your body and self-care. You will be guided to *be* and *do.* △ **Air** is *abstract and rational.* It embodies the mind, thoughts, and ideas. Air is our breath, our connection to the Universe, and communication. It is the wind that shapes our character. Air has qualities of positivity, direction, and empowerment. If you draw an Air card, use your *thoughts* to transform. △ **Fire** is *activating and arousing.* It represents light and heat, clarity and vision. Fire is vitality and vigor, creativity, and strength. Fire has qualities of purification, refinement, and brilliance. If you draw a Fire card, the message is a call to action and to look at things differently. Get busy and find your guidance in *action.* ▽ **Water** is *emotional and intuitive.* It represents fluidity and cooling. Water is the soul contained within the body, our heart, and the womb of Life. Water has qualities of transparency, penetrability, and mirroring. If you draw a Water card, your transformations will come from deep inside your heart. Let your *feelings* guide you.

ORIGINS OF THE ELEMENTS IN THE I-CHING

The ancient Book of Changes, the I-Ching, has 8 signs distributed among the 4 elements, as follows:

EARTH ▽		
yin, receptive, cold, dark individuality, resilience acted upon by other forces	☷	**Earth** | The Receptive
	☶	**Mountain** | Keeping Still

AIR △		
awakening, slow growth spreading & circulating sustaining, roots & branches	☴	**Wind** | The Gentle
	☳	**Thunder** | The Arousing

FIRE △		
yang, active, hot, light strong outside but soft inside clarity, rapid movement	☲	**Fire** | The Clinging
	☰	**Heaven** | The Creative

WATER ▽		
soft outside but strong inside heart & soul slow transformation	☵	**Water** | The Abysmal
	☱	**Lake** | The Joyous

EARTH

BODY

material possessions | health | home | wealth

The Earth element governs the material, the physical, and the sensual. A *passive* element, Earth allows growth, production, harvest, and recycling. It promotes prosperity, but also its opposites of decay and diminishment. Earth forms the foundation on which everything can be built, and to which all ruins return.

MOVEMENT

DOWN

FORM

rock | stone | crystal | humus | mud | clay | sand | dust

ACTIONS & PROPERTIES

grounding · centering · stabilizing · down-to-earth
molding · sculpting · digging · excavating · extracting
fertile · plowing · planting · raking · producing
yielding · receiving · passive · forgiving
quaking · burying · humbling · recycling
recording · revealing · reliable · supporting

MIND

thought patterns | philosophy | truth | ideas

The Air element governs intellect, logic, reasoning, and communication. An *active* element, Air circulates and so cleanses. Air carries our thoughts and dreams. Like the sky, our mind or thoughts can be clear or clouded, ruffled by inner winds of confusion, or calmed by the stillness of meditation. Speech requires breath, which requires Air.

MOVEMENT

UP

FORM

sky | wind | cloud | breeze | oxygen | breath | weather

ACTIONS & PROPERTIES

life-giving · breathing · inspiring · vitalizing
lifting · carrying · dispersing · sailing · flying
circulating · swirling · sweeping · reforming · spreading
blowing · screaming · bellowing · amplifying
clearing · unpredictable · ubiquitous
goes anywhere, in any direction

 △ FIRE

SPIRIT

soul path | action | ambition | creativity | divine light

The Fire element is all about energy and action. Fire ignites passion, willpower, drive, and ambition. It brings the light of clarity, illuminates the soul's path, and shines the way on our journey. Fire is an *active* element, causing permanent change, especially related to old behavior patterns. Fire energy is expansive. It can be aggressive, pro-active, and unstoppable.

MOVEMENT

UP

FORM

sun | stars | candlelight | campfire | sparks | electricity

ACTIONS & PROPERTIES

guiding · revealing · clarifying · illuminating · blinding
heating · baking · cooking · warming · comforting
burning · scorching · drying · consuming · destroying
passionate · visionary · higher consciousness
motivating · electrifying · animating

WATER

HEART

feelings | emotions | intuition | love | faith

The heart is like the ocean, moving in tides. Waves of feeling can rise and fall. Water is a *passive* element. It can be deep or shallow. When water is out of control, the emotions overflow in a flood. Feelings and intuitions can meander like branches in a river, surging forward. Feelings can also be frozen like ice, shut down.

MOVEMENT

DOWN

FORM

ocean | lake | river | waterfall | rain | swamp | glacier

ACTIONS & PROPERTIES

cleansing · washing · dissolving · spreading · stirring
flooding · eroding · overflowing · drowning · dredging
weeping · leaking · seeping · pouring · drenching
storming · showering · renewing · refreshing · quenching
conveying · carrying · transporting · drifting
unconsciousness · floating · diving in

GETTING STARTED

CALL ON SPIRIT

When you first open your *Transformation Oracle*, take a moment to bless it and ask for its mystical powers to become part of your life.

Using the oracle cards is simple: become quiet inside. Ask the Universe for clarity and direction. *Focus on a meaningful question about your life and become very present.* Be aware of your sensations, feelings, visions, and thoughts. Then open your heart for guidance and shuffle the cards face down. Sometimes a card "jumps" out of the deck with a special message for you. Each card you draw is aligned to that moment.

SET A CLEAR INTENTION

Align with Spirit in your own way.

Before a reading, be sure you are *grounded* and *centered*.

Connect with the Divine in whatever way works for you: e.g., Great Spirit; God; Universal Healing Powers; Archangels Michael, Gabriel, Raphael, Uriel, etc. Call upon the Divine in your own way to *open a connection*.

Ask for the *highest good* to flow through the readings. Humbly ask to be a clear channel, with no impediment, blockage, or ego that might get in the way of the message coming through. When you are ready, begin!

SHUFFLING

There are dozens of ways to shuffle cards. With the *Transformation Oracle,* no particular way is "right" or "wrong." Use the method that feels best to connect with your own intuitive abilities. Here are a few popular ways to shuffle the cards.

OVERHAND SHUFFLE

1. Place the long edge of the deck in one palm.
2. Lift about half the deck off the stack.
3. Lightly release a small number of cards into the deck.
4. Continue until all cards are released.

RIFFLE SHUFFLE

1. Split the deck in half.
2. Take ½ in each hand.
3. Using your thumbs, middle fingers, and pinkies, bend the cards and riffle the two halves together.
4. Bend the cards the opposite way to cascade and consolidate.
5. Repeat.

SCRAMBLE SHUFFLE

1. Lay the deck face down on a large table surface.
2. Using both hands, stir the cards as though smearing paint.
3. Collect the cards back into a deck and select one.

PICKING CARDS

PICK FROM AN ARRAY

1. Gently spread the deck out in a row, face down
2. Using your fingertips, scan your hand slowly over the cards until you sense your card
3. Slip the card from the spread, being sure it slides out easily
4. If your card seems "stuck" or clings to adjacent cards, release it and scan for another

DEALER-STYLE: FROM THE TOP

1. Cut the cards
2. Place deck face down
3. Create your spread by picking each card consecutively from the top of the deck

TOUCH AND GO

1. Hold the deck face-down in both hands
2. Sort through the face-down deck using the fingertips of both hands
3. Concentrate on the meaning of the first position in your spread
4. Use the fingertips of either hand to sense the first card
5. Continue with each position in the spread, holding its meaning or
   intention to find each successive card

DIVINE GUIDANCE

Sometimes the cards have "a mind of their own." Here is what they are trying to tell us.

CARDS THAT "POP" OR "JUMP" OUT

When cards fall, pop, or jump from the deck unintentionally, Spirit is showing us our cards rather than waiting for us to pick! Popping cards have special messages Spirit wants us to see. Cards may pop out for certain people every time they read; others may never have cards pop, fall, or jump. If no cards pop, simply use your preferred picking method. There is no "good" or "bad" about how we communicate with Spirit through the oracle.

REVERSED CARDS

Reversed, inverted, or upside-down cards indicate resistance or difficulty. Often, it's a matter of the timing being too early or too late. Reversed cards also signify denial, avoidance, lack of awareness, or compromise. Check the card's page in this guidebook for its reversed meaning.

REPEATING CARDS

We may notice a certain card comes up over and over again, especially when reading for ourselves. A repeating card is the oracle telling us that message is still in the spotlight! Professional readers often see a certain card repeating when that issue is highlighted because of astrological, political, or spiritual circumstances.

WHY ARE THERE 44 CARDS?

The Spirit Guides behind the *Transformation Oracle* wanted it based on the master number 44, the number of intuition and inner wisdom. This number doubles the vibrations of the number 4, which concerns establishing solid foundations for yourself and others to create wholeness, worthiness, and success.

Each of the four elements has 11 cards. The number 11 is the first master number, metaphysically speaking. This number is extremely powerful to higher intuition and spiritual insight. Mentally and physically, 11 points to deep sensitivity, empathy, intuition, and intelligence—the exact qualities of Light Workers and oracle card readers! The doubling of 1 is a key to infinity and unlocking the secrets of the Universe.

Master number 44 points to reliability, stability, and perseverance. This number equips us to handle all challenges, as it reinforces the qualities of responsibility, discipline, imagination, and inner calmness. The full deck brings great blessings and support to all who use it for connection with the Divine Mystery of life.

ARE THERE ANY "BAD" CARDS?

In the *Transformation Oracle*, each situation contains helpful lessons. There is no evil omen or warning of misfortune and disaster. The energies involved combine together to create various situations and environments for our spiritual growth. In life, we each go through changes and lessons. Some circumstances can feel difficult or challenging on many levels. Rather than being "bad," such situations often open us to the grace of deep spiritual transformation.

I'M SCARED TO KNOW THE FUTURE . . .

The *Transformation Oracle* is different from more ancient divination systems like the Tarot, which was used for centuries for fortune telling and portending the future. This oracle is a contemporary tool for personal and spiritual growth. Because it is a Light Worker's deck, the *Transformation Oracle* is meant to bring deeper understanding of life circumstances, rather than portend dark omens of the future. It is designed to reveal which forces are at work to create change in your life. Many changes are underfoot now, and you will see like an x-ray what's going on underneath. For example, the **Element Balancing** spread, which was channeled with this deck, simply shows what is happening in each of the four elements. These changes relate easily to the aspects of body, heart, mind, and spirit.

Working with the *Transformation Oracle* is like looking in a metaphysical mirror. We get a deeper, more revealing picture of ourselves. The perspective we get from the oracle is not necessarily linear: the future is not always different from the present! In other words, the forces at work are sometimes large and slow-moving. We may have to repeat certain patterns and situations over and over before we can truly transform them—and ourselves.

Cards can only imply the future based on current tendencies. Your own future is not written until *you* write your part!

READING FOR OTHERS

Using divination cards is everything from a fun pastime with friends and family to a lucrative career. If we read for others, we can ask ourselves: What is my intention with the *Transformation Oracle*? Amusement? Personal growth? Divination for others? A profession?

CLARIFY THE ROLES

If we are playing, let's have fun! Skip ahead to the Spreads, or just jump in and read cards.

If we do sincere or paid readings for others, this section guides us towards a Divinely connected approach. Oracle cards may be our main tool or an accessory we consult occasionally.

Whether amateur or professional, our divination can have a powerful effect on the *seeker*. Most seekers have passionate feelings about their questions. After all, these are matters of health, love, family, money, employment, housing: all the big issues in life!

As a *reader*, our talents and gifts—sometimes called our "clairs" (for clairvoyance, clairaudience, etc.) are vital to interpreting messages from the Divine. Either way, the impression we make may fall into a spectrum whose ends prompt the seeker either to become a lifelong return customer, or to permanently abandon divination. It's not uncommon for a reading to have a life-altering affect on the seeker. How we understand our role and the way we use words to interpret can make all the difference.

THE PROFESSIONAL READER'S JOB

- To interpret messages from Spirit
- To give advice, guidance, direction
- To help the seeker on her/his path
- To maintain authority & credibility
- To respond to questions & concerns
- To provide a safe, reliable source of information

STAY IN THE LIGHT

If you read at fairs, parties, or as part of your daily work, remember to leave enough time to clear your deck and reconnect to Spirit between readings. It's easy to get affected by the energies our seekers bring in. Clearing the deck and ourselves ensures that our readings are tuned into the will of the Divine.

PROTECT YOUR LANGUAGE

Our choice of words and phrases can make or break how seekers respond to a reading. This chart shows two contrasting approaches to wording. Which do you prefer when others read for you? Which do you use in reading?

Antagonizing	Empathizing
Puts people on the defensive	*Neutralizes, puts people at ease*
Bossy, patronizing	Respectful, collaborative
You need to …	Have you considered …
You/he/she should …	Perhaps you're already …
You have to …	If I may suggest …
Why don't you just …	Might it be an option to …

PRAYERS

BEFORE A READING

Great Spirit, I call on You to be with me now.

I humbly offer myself as Your servant for ____________'s highest good. Let me be a clear and open channel for Your light, Your healing, and Your love.

May all my words, intuitive thoughts, and interpretations radiate Your intentions for ____________.

Thank you for my gifts as a reader and for letting me serve You and ____________ in this way. Amen.

BETWEEN READINGS

Great Spirit,

I call on You to cleanse, heal, shield, and protect me now.

Please guard all my channels of communication with Your Divine Light, so I may serve Your Highest Good.

Guide me, remove whatever in me stands in the way of Your Perfect Guidance, that I might serve my Seeker according to your Divine Will & Blessing. Thank You for this Grace.   Amen.

CLEANSING THE CARDS

RESET THE DECK

1. Count the cards (especially at shows!). Make sure there are 44.
2. Turn all cards upright (none reversed).
3. Sort the deck into the four elements.
4. Arrange each element into its original order, using the chart on page 149.

KNOCK THE CARDS

1. Gather the cards into a tight pack.
2. Hold the deck facing downward in your non-dominant hand.
3. Make a fist with your dominant hand and knock the cards sharply a couple times to shake out old energy and neutralize.

SHUFFLE THE DECK

1. Using whichever technique you prefer, shuffle the deck until you feel it has been cleared of old energy & neutralized.
2. Loosen up. Surrender any sense of attachment to a particular outcome.

CLEAR THE DECK

1. Use a crystal or pendulum to eliminate old energy, neutralize, and revitalize the deck in a short time.
2. Clear quartz, amethyst, kyanite, apophylite, and celestite are good cleansers & quickly dispel negative or residual energy.

"DEEP CLEANSE" VISUALIZATION

1. Hold the card deck in both hands at arm's length. Visualize your aura as light all around you, as wide as your arms reach.
2. Keep your elbows straight and sweep the deck through your aura. Begin overhead, moving the deck in an arc from high to low and side to side.
3. Starting at your solar plexus, sweep the deck outward, straightening your arms, then bring it back to your core.
4. Continue sweeping the deck, spinning in a circle or using spiral motions to cleanse the deck. Continue to visualize your aura as a brilliant ball of light all around you.
5. Hold the deck at your heart, third eye, or solar plexus.
6. Visualize white light streaming down from the Divine through your deck, cleaning out old energies, biases, and impurities from past readings.

For more insights on working with the *Transformation Oracle*, please visit: **transformation-oracle.com**

THE SPREADS

HOW TO LAY OUT AND READ CARDS

INTERPRETING PHASES OF TRANSFORMATION

SINGLE CARD

for daily guidance

HOW TO

1. Focus on your question.
2. Shuffle the cards.
3. Pick or find the card that "calls" to you.

Trust Your Intuition

4. Read the card name: what does this word evoke?
5. Scan the artwork: what do you observe? Consider the imagery, colors, symbols, geometry, and so on.

Delve Deeper

6. Use this Guide Book—all cards are listed in alphabetical order.
7. Use the Website: simply type the URL *transformation-oracle.com/* (remember the forward slash!), followed by your card name for an online version: e.g. *transformation-oracle.com/journey.*
8. Refer to previous readings: what have you learned?

YOU ARE THE KEY!

Your own understandings and interpretations are vital to readings! Take a moment to grow your confidence by considering your:

- Expertise | Life Experience
- Bodies of Knowledge, Studies & Interests
- Psychic Talents & Reading Style: Empath? Intuitive?
- Whether harnessed or yet undiscovered, your Gifts of:
  clairvoyance—seeing mystical visions or patterns
  clairaudience—hearing celestial music, words & voices
  claircognizance—divine or prophetic knowing
  clairsentience—feeling presences when no one is there

TRANSFORMATION

The essence of this Oracle is Transformation. Your own story and journey of spiritual growth and change is at the heart of your interpretation for yourself and others:

- All symbols in the cards serve **transformation**
- Each card intersects many knowledge bases & systems
- Topics appear according to the way they were channeled
- Many cards fit several concepts simultaneously
- Each card potentially has infinite interpretations based on the spread, seeker,
  reader, and current situation

Always read a card's element FIRST.
Find an orientation in body, heart, mind & spirit.
Ground your interpretation through these basic principles.

PAST-PRESENT-FUTURE

Use an arc of time to zero in on a single issue. The amount of time can be as small as a day, where morning is past, noon is present, and night is future. It can be several years, or even many lifetimes.

HOW TO

1. Set your intention and shuffle the cards.

2. Select 3 cards and place them face down, as shown in the diagram on the next page.
   The first card represents the Present.
   The left card represents the Past.
   The right card represents the Future.
3. Turn over one card at a time, starting with the Present.

4. Notice the *element* of each card:
   ▽ **Earth** (body & material possessions)
   △ **Air** (thoughts & ideas)
   ▽ **Water** (heart, feelings, emotions)
   △ **Fire** (spiritual growth, action)

5. Observe how the issue has shifted over time.

BASIC LAYOUT & CARD ORDER

QUESTIONS

What will happen with __________ ?
What went on with __________ ?

TOPICS

relationship | health | home | career | wealth | projects

For example readings of this and other spreads,
go to: **transformation-oracle.com**

YES | NO | MAYBE

for quick, clear guidance

HOW TO

1. Focus on your question.
2. Shuffle the cards.
3. Pick 3 cards and place them in the order shown.
4. Turn over the top card first, reading its element.
5. "Open" the bottom two cards together, like barn doors and read their elements.
6. Read the individual card meanings for deeper insights.

QUESTIONS

Is it in my highest good to do __________ ?
Is it advisable to __________ ?
Is it the highest good for all if I __________ ?
Is it best for __________ if I say __________ ?
Will __________ happen?
Will __________ happen next (time frame) __________ ?

YES

The top element matches one or both bottom elements, shown at left and middle.

If all three elements match, as shown at far right, it is considered an "absolute yes," divined by Spirit. With an "absolute yes," we can be certain and trust the outcome!

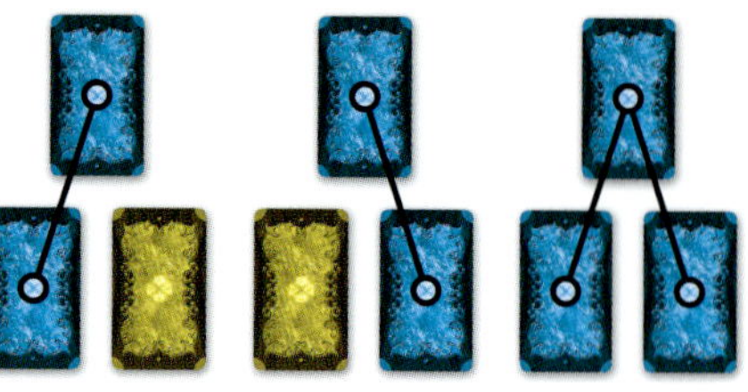

NO

The bottom elements match, shown at right. The top element is different. Here, Spirit clearly guides us with the answer, "no."

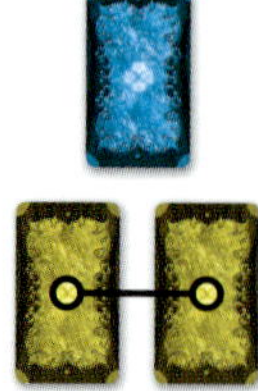

MAYBE

None of the elements match. All three elements are different. "Maybe" doesn't mean "Yes" and it doesn't mean "No." Read the individual cards to see which way the outcome may go.

TIP Try to *accept* your answer, even if you don't "like" it. Asking too many Yes/No/Maybe questions clouds the issue. Try a deeper spread for insights.

LEVELS OF BEING

to align your path

This spread shown on the next page was channeled for the *Transformation Oracle*. The situation reads from inner to outer, starting with yourself and moving towards the Divine. A quick view of your **path** shows you where you are heading. The bottom card represents you, today, in this moment. The middle card expands on your circumstances, including community and culture. The top card shows the outcome or potential of all factors combined.

Think of the cards as radiating out from you or your seeker (bottom), through others / the environment (middle), to the destiny or outcome (top).

ANCIENT ROOTS IN THE I-CHING

The ancient I-Ching's hexagrams read from the bottom upward and from inner (individual | personal) to outer (social | world).

In a hexagram, the lower trigram reveals the inner situation, while the upper trigram shows the outer.

In a single trigram, the levels of consciousness increase from the mundane | physical, up through the social, to the spiritual at the top.

HOW TO

1. Shuffle the cards, concentrating on your situation.
2. When you are ready, pull 3 cards.
3. Lay the cards bottom to top, as shown at right.
4. Read the cards, letting intuition speak to you.

  - The **bottom card** (closest to you) shows what's going on with you, what you are focused on.
  - The **middle card** reveals the support you can expect from people in your community including family, friends, coworkers, or your significant relationship. It also indicates the broader spectrum of time, history, politics, and outer conditions.
  - The **top card** shows your destiny or outcome.

5. Notice the flow of *elements* in the spread. What pattern do you see? How does this relate to your experience?

3
OUTCOME
DESTINY

2
SUPPORT
OTHERS
ENVIRONMENT

1
YOU

TIP Consider how the Phases of Transformation come into play in this spread. What do you observe?

ELEMENT BALANCING

The Element Balancing spread was channeled with the *Transformation Oracle*. It is a quick way to get an x-ray on a situation and see what is "up."

Working with the elements gives you very quick insight into which aspects and areas of life are concerned. This "shortcut" gives extra insights into your readings and helps quickly establish rapport with the seeker.

HOW TO

1. Shuffle the deck and when you're ready pull 4 cards.
2. Place the cards clockwise and face up, as shown.
3. Focus on each card's *element*. If your spread has all four elements, you're balanced!
   - ▽ **Earth** / body • possessions, home, health
   - ▽ **Water** / heart • feelings, intuition, relationship
   - △ **Air** / mind • thoughts, philosophy, attitudes
   - △ **Fire** / spirit • energy, activation, life vision

Go for fine-tuning. If all cards are from the same element, that area of your life needs special attention. You either have too much or too little of that element. If you get 2-3 cards from one element, notice the theme of what's *repeated* or *missing*. Say a prayer and draw another card for guidance on how to *balance* your relationship to the four elements. Look for subtle messages in the artwork's mystical symbols.

BASIC LAYOUT & CARD ORDER

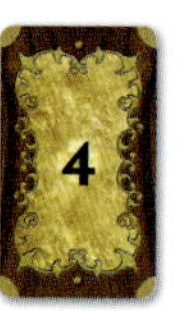

BALANCED

- *All four elements are present*

When all four elements appear in the spread, the situation is balanced.
Read each card for individual guidance in body, heart, mind & spirit.

EMPHASIS

• *Three elements are present*

If two cards are in the same element, the situation is basically balanced with an *emphasis* in one aspect of being.

DOUBLE EMPHASIS

• *Two elements are present, both doubled*

If only two elements appear in the spread and both are doubled, there is emphasis on *both* of those areas.

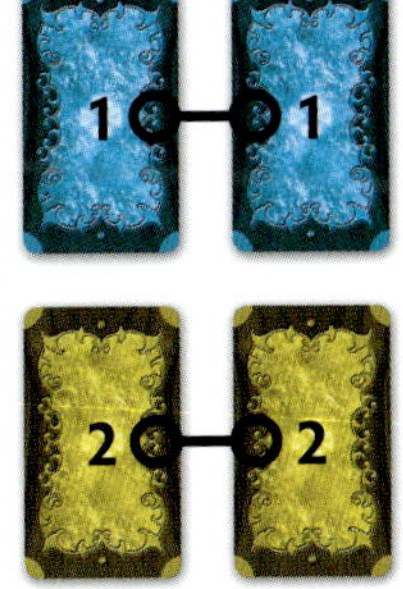

FOCUS

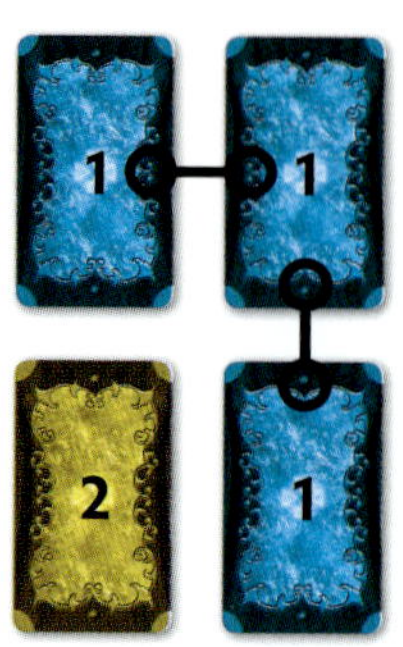

• *Two elements are present*

When three cards are in one element, there is a strong *focus* on that aspect of being. This situation shows a *degree* of over-emphasis or imbalance.

IMBALANCED

• *Only one element is present*

If all four cards are in the same element, the situation is imbalanced by too much or too little of one element. Sometimes imbalance is necessary in moving forward...!

ELEMENT BALANCING WITH PLAYING CARDS

A deck of regular playing cards can be used for the Element Balancing spread. Follow the instructions above to read the elements in regular playing cards.

Suited Cards

There are four suits in regular playing cards, corresponding to the four elements as follows:

Diamonds – Earth ▽   body: wealth, health, home
Spades – Air △   mind: ideas, thoughts, philosophy
Hearts – Water ▽   heart: feelings, intuition, faith
Clubs – Fire △   spirit: action, soul path, creativity

TIP   For example readings of this spread, go to: **transformation-oracle.com**

ELEMENT BALANCING WITH TAROT CARDS

Identify the element of each card using this chart.

Minor Arcana (Suited Cards)

Pentacles	Earth ▽	Swords	Air △
Cups	Water ▽	Wands	Fire △

Major Arcana (Figure Cards)

▽ Earth Cards

3	The Empress
5	The Hierophant
9	The Hermit
15	The Devil
21	The World

▽ Water Cards

2	The High Priestess
7	The Chariot
12	The Hanged Man
13	Death
18	The Moon

△ Air Cards

0	The Fool
1	The Magician
6	The Lovers
11	Justice
17	The Star

△ Fire Cards

4	The Emperor
8	Strength
10	The Wheel of Fortune
14	Temperance
16	The Tower
19	The Sun
20	Judgment

PROJECT SPREAD

for large endeavors

Imagine the spread space divided in half down the middle. The left side represents *human effort and intention* in the project. The right side represents *worldly effect and Divine will* for the outcome.

HOW TO

1. Shuffle the cards, then lay the first card at the bottom left.
2. Continue to place two more cards above the first, similar to the **Levels of Being** spread.
3. Move to the bottom right and place another three cards in a column, starting from the bottom.
4. Read the cards for the project's status from beginning, through middle, to end.

WHEN TO USE

- Before beginning a project
- After completing a project, before outcome is known
- At any point in the middle of a project

TOPICS & PROJECTS

business ventures | wealth management

education & assignments | crafts & creative work

recovery | fitness & health

building | expansion | renovation

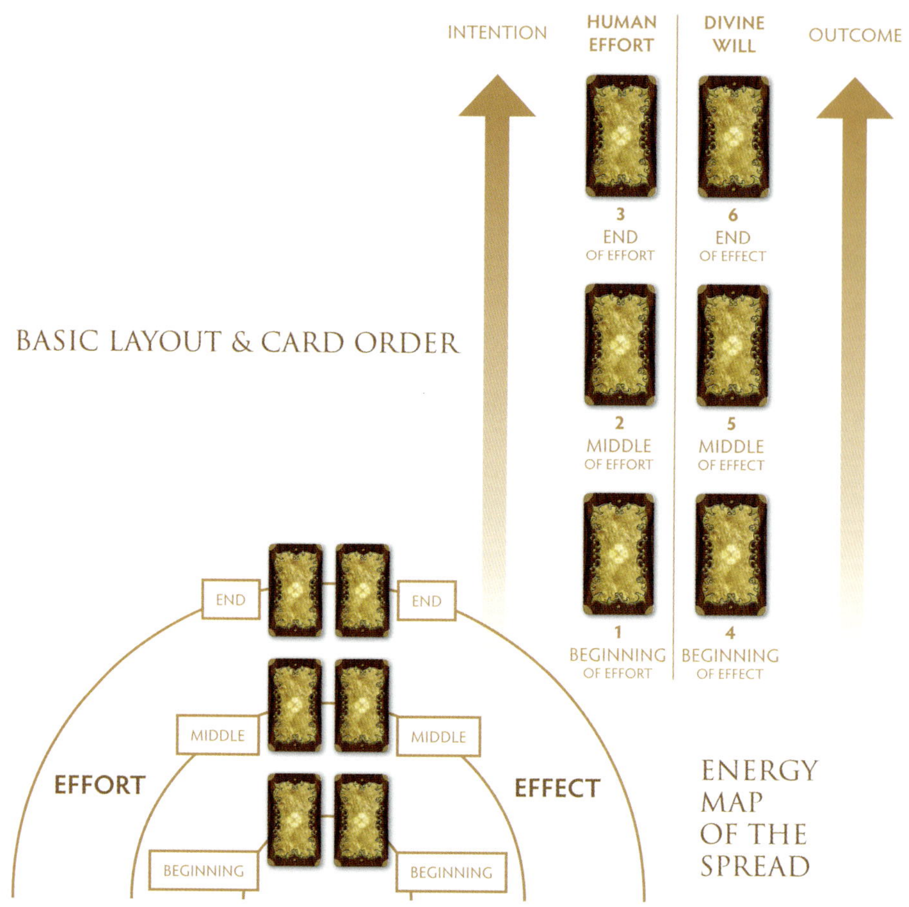

BASIC LAYOUT & CARD ORDER
INTENTION
HUMAN EFFORT
DIVINE WILL
OUTCOME
3
END OF EFFORT
6
END OF EFFECT
2
MIDDLE OF EFFORT
5
MIDDLE OF EFFECT
1
BEGINNING OF EFFORT
4
BEGINNING OF EFFECT
END
END
MIDDLE
MIDDLE
BEGINNING
BEGINNING
EFFORT
EFFECT
ENERGY MAP OF THE SPREAD

RELATIONSHIP SPREAD

for relationships

HOW TO

Follow the directions for the **Element Balancing** spread, creating one spread for each person.
1. Read the element balance for each person separately. Then read the elements and cards in the relationship. Which elements are shared between the two people? Where is there conflict?
2. This spread can be used to read for family and group dynamics. It expands to include all sorts of relationship structures, including political, social, and spiritual.

WHEN TO USE

- When conflicts arise
- For communication problems
- For insights on relationship dynamics and differences

RELATIONSHIPS

spouse | lover | dating prospect

parent | child | sibling | relative | friend

boss | employee | partner | candidate

student | teacher | administrator

vendor | supplier | organizer

leader | community | congregation | civilians

PERSON 1   PERSON 2

PARENT   CHILD

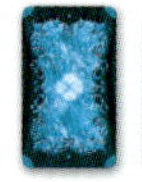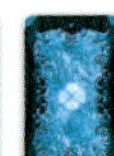

LEADER   CIVILIANS

EXPANDING A SPREAD

Expanding a spread means pulling additional cards to deepen your insights and readings. The extra cards can follow one axis of the spread, such as time or psychology. You can also expand by pulling one or more extra cards at any location in the spread. The expansion gives extra information to the reading, clarifying details.

WHEN TO USE

- More information is needed
- Past lives or memories surface
- Conditions are uncertain or unclear

HOW TO

We learned the horizontal axis of time (left to right) in the **Past, Present, Future** spread. Add a card on either end to widen the span of time.

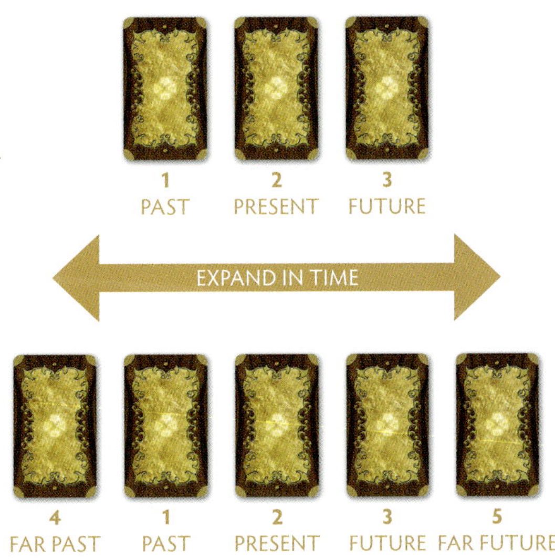

Using the vertical axis (up and down) add a card above and below. You can read Above as the Divine, the higher self, or the superconscious mind. The Below shows the base motivations, the lower self, or the unconscious mind

Expand in both directions for a matrix of insight.

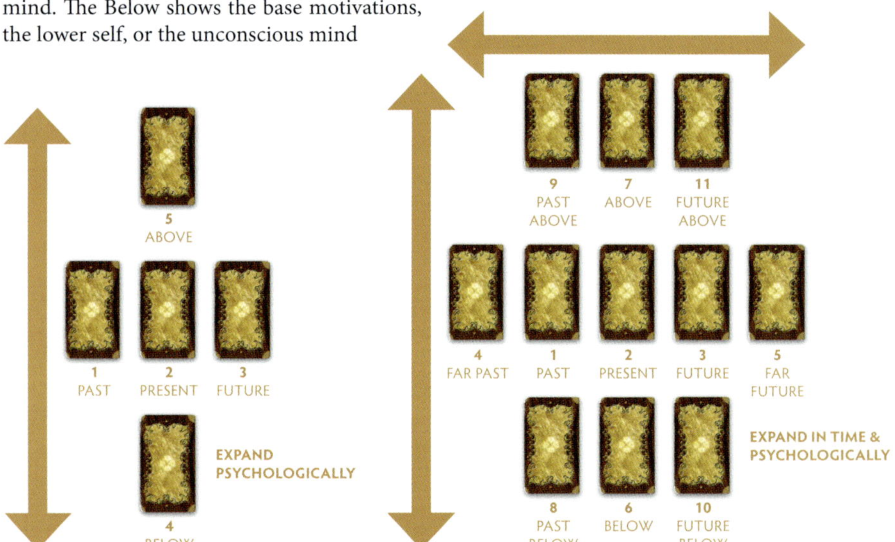

CHAKRA SPREAD

for in-depth insights

This advanced spread rests on our knowledge of **Chakras**, the centers of spiritual power in Indian thought. The seven chakras relate to our central nervous system as well as to concepts of mature identity and destiny. This spread should be used on adults, whose chakras are fully grown. We read each card according to our knowledge of the chakras as a key to spiritual health.

WHEN TO USE

- When many issues are "up" all at once
- During major life transitions
- When element balancing isn't enough
- To confirm or uncover a life purpose, karma & destiny

CHAKRA CHECKLIST

1 Root | *I am*

2 Sacral | *I feel*

3 Solar Plexus | *I do*

4 Heart | *I love*

5 Throat | *I speak*

6 Third Eye | *I see*

7 Crown | *I understand*

TIP For example readings of this spread, go to: **transformation-oracle.com**

BASIC LAYOUT

HOW TO

The Chakra Spread is highly intentional and intuitive. Drawing upon your knowledge of the Chakras and your intuition about the seeker, begin drawing cards in the order that feels right to you:

- Start at the heart, then alternate progressively outward
- Start with the heart, root, and crown, then fill in the other chakras
- One by one from the root up to the crown
- One by one from the crown down to the root
- In the intuitive and intentional order that comes to you

FIND THE KEY

Each Chakra spread is different. Look for a key to unlock the secret codes:

- Which elements are present? Missing?
- Can you see a pattern in element locations by Chakra?
- Does one card leap out at you? What is its Chakra?

CELTIC CROSS

for in-depth insights

This ancient spread comes from the Piscean Age. With insights into time, situation, and outcome, the Celtic Cross remains a perpetually helpful spread to memorize for deeper readings.

Because it is well-traveled, there are many variations on how to do the Celtic Cross. Here is one we recommend for the *Transformation Oracle*. Please use the variant of your preference.

HOW TO

Shuffle the deck. Place and read the cards *face-up* as follows:

1. The Present (situation and state of mind / perception)
2. The Challenge (problem or obstacle)
3. The Past (how it got this way)
4. The Future (next step)
5. What is Below (subconscious, what's at the core of the situation)
6. What is Above (conscious goal)
7. Advice (recommended approach)
8. Influences (people, energies, and events beyond the seeker's control)
9. Hopes and Fears (all mixed together)
10. The Outcome (resolution)

WHEN TO USE

- For deep insights into a situation
- For a forecast on birthdays and anniversaries
- As a basic spread when reading for clients

BASIC LAYOUT &
CARD ORDER

6

ABOVE

3

PAST

2
CHALLENGE

1

PRESENT

4

FUTURE

5

BELOW

10

OUTCOME

9

HOPES
& FEARS

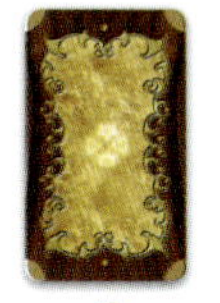

8

INFLUENCES

7

ADVICE

PHASES OF TRANSFORMATION

Once we are fluent in the elements, cards, and basic spreads, there's a shortcut into our readings. The transformations in this Oracle can be broken into different stages or *phases*. Reinforcing our psychic abilities, knowing the phases give us quick insight to the seeker's situation. For example, a **Beginning** card tells us that the seeker is starting something new. Knowing and identifying the phases accelerates our accuracy.

Many theories explain spiritual growth, such as the hero's journey, sacred rites of passage, or stages of ascension and mastery. The *Transformation Oracle* has eight phases. Some phases have more cards than others. These phases are nonlinear transitory events. Different phases of transformation happen simultaneously in a single person. Life is a complex process and spiritual evolution is multi-dimensional. Phases give us landmarks to way-find and deepen our interpretations.

TIP Duality cards are marked with an asterisk (*). Read more on page 55.

TIP For examples of how to interpret the phases of transformation, go to: **transformation-oracle.com**

BEGINNING

Rite of Passage | New School | Career Change
Graduation | Retirement
Travel | Embarking | Moving
New Love | Marriage | Parenthood

JOURNEY   TRICKSTER   TEMPTATION   EMERGENCE

REBIRTH   INITIATION   INNOCENCE   RESURRECTION *

The eight Beginning cards reveal that something new is afoot. If one of these cards appears in a spread, it acts as a door to open the spread. A Beginning card can guide how we interpret the other cards. The new beginning cues our understanding of the seeker's situation.

ENDING

HARVEST

SEPARATION *

REVERSAL *

RENOVATION

RESOLUTION

CELEBRATION

The six Ending cards indicate that the seeker is in closure and termination. Some ending cards reveal a happy ending, while others awaken us to the seeker's possible loss or grief. Some Endings imply new beginnings while others are messy or inconclusive.

STASIS

Inactivity | Standing Still | Stagnation
Waiting | Indecision | Spinning Wheels

We see that the seeker is lost or stuck in Stasis cards.

DIRECTION

STUCK

QUIETUDE

Calmness | Peace | Rejuvenation | Restoration
Meditation | Seeking the Divine | Stillness

Quietude cards show self-care and spiritual gifts.

CONTEMPLATION

REST

PRAYER

INTUITION

GROWTH

Progress | Expansion | Breakthrough | Pregnancy
Acquisition | Increase | Major Shift in Power

DISCOVERY   KNOWLEDGE   STRATEGY *   LIBERATION

STRENGTHEN   QUICKENING   EXPANSION

The seven Growth cards help us read the seeker's ambitions and pursuits. Often a seeker is already well underway with growth energy when these cards appear in a spread. As readers we can encourage the seeker, pointing out the details of how to stimulate, reinforce, or increase growth.

NOURISHMENT

Divine Blessings & Support | Gifts | Endowments

Legacy | Inheritance | Spiritual Funding

Nourishment cards imply gratitude and blessings.

GENEROSITY *   GRACE   CREATIVITY   CONNECTION

DECLINE

Deterioration | Diminishment | Loss | Release

Darkening of the Light | Dark Night of the Soul

Decline cards show changed circumstances and power.

DESCENT   SIMPLICITY   SURRENDER

REFINEMENT

Improvement | Conditioning | Limitation

Cleansing | Removing Impurities

Polishing | Finishing | Acquisition of Style or Culture

The ten cards in the Refinement phase, as shown on page 56, indicate work on the self that may take a long time to process. Unlike Beginning and Ending cards, which can be short-term phases of transformation, the Refinement cards show us the backbone of our personal growth. These processes take repetition, discipline, and time. Some Refinement cards involve mystical ideas, such as the reclaiming of lost experience and effort in Recycle and Immigration, the transmutation of emotional stains in Purification and Forgiveness, and the naked self-honesty of Reflection or the vigilance required in Ascent and Wisdom. Receptivity and Integration cause us to look at the complexity of our inner environments, clearing and ordering them so we can serve our highest purpose.

DUALITY CARDS

Six Duality cards, marked by an asterisk (*) show situations that can go one of two ways:

Immigration	Old vs. New | Familiar vs. Strange (page 87)
Separation	Termination vs. Enmeshment (page 129)
Resurrection	Yes vs. No | Viable vs. Non-viable (page 125)
Reversal	Ascent vs. Decline (page 127)
Generosity	Give vs. Receive (page 81)
Strategy	Advance vs. Retreat (page 133)

RECYCLE

FORGIVENESS

RECEPTIVITY

IMMIGRATION *

INTEGRATION

ASCENT

WISDOM

PURIFICATION

REFLECTION

PERSPECTIVE

YOUR TRANSFORMATION JOURNEY

The Phases of Transformation affect us all. As you use the *Transformation Oracle*, certain cards will sing out to you. These cards seem brighter and more powerful than others, because they are part of *your* transformation experience.

QUESTIONS TO EXPLORE

- Which *element* do you consider as yours?
  Why?
- Is there an *element* you can't relate to easily?
  Why not?
- Which *cards* resonate most with your experience of Transformation?
  Consider cards in **Earth, Air, Fire,** and **Water**.
- Which cards are most *difficult* for you to connect with? Why?
- Which phase(s) of Transformation are you in today?
  Which cards best express your experience now?
- When you consider the Phases of Transformation, which one(s) stands out
    as having affected you the most in your life so far?
- In which *element* is your card?
  What does it say about you?

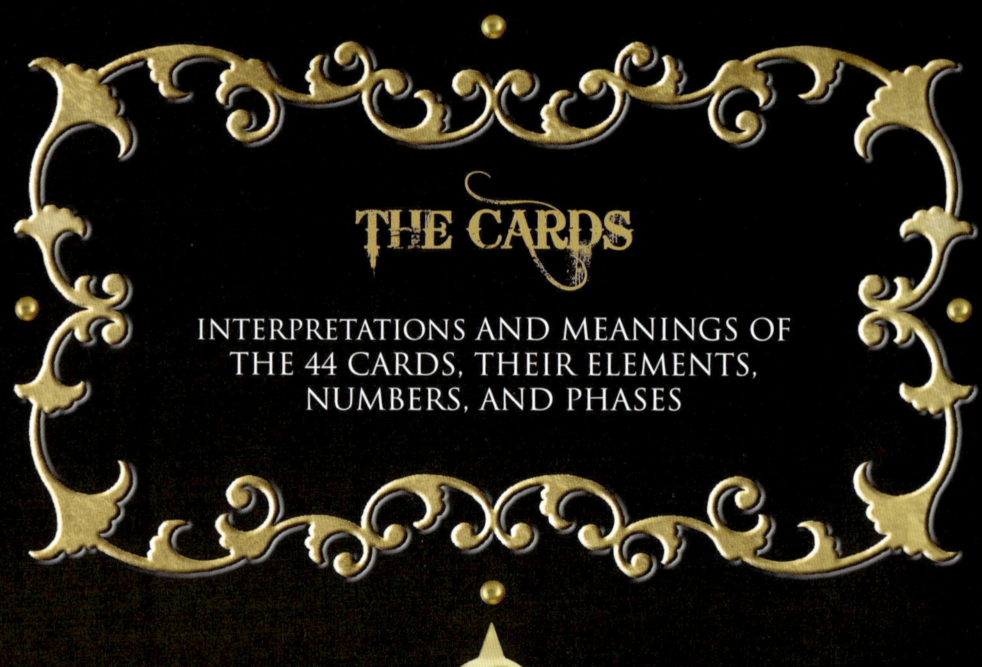

THE CARDS

INTERPRETATIONS AND MEANINGS OF THE 44 CARDS, THEIR ELEMENTS, NUMBERS, AND PHASES

ASCENT

Rise up to higher ground!
Let your opponents fall
away below.

When facing a challenge, do your best to rise above negativity. Hold your head high! Battles with others abound, and we are certain to lose our share. Don't settle for inner weakness. Discouragement, anger, and depression are the easy way out. Instead, look for the positive. Write a gratitude list of everything good in your life: health, family and friends, work, Nature—even small acts of kindness directed toward you. Then you will **ascend.**

Know that whomever behaved badly towards you is trapped in a darkness, fear, and lovelessness. The saying, *"Just like me!"* reminds us that, at times, we are no better than others. Find compassion for yourself at your worst, so you can extend it to "enemies." Let your opponents fall away below you. Leave them to their bad behavior while you go forth in grace. Model how to rise above pettiness and greed with courtesy and dignity.

Life is a jagged road. Ignore the unsupportive words and actions of others by casting negativity from your mind. Keep climbing toward the Light. Take with you those who are ready to reach new heights and let yourself fly!

ARTWORK:

"Above The Jealous Mouths"

ELEMENT: △ AIR   NUMBER: **9**   PHASE: **REFINEMENT**

DEEPER INSIGHTS

*The warrior straddles an amethyst cliff
above a ruined battleground.*

Symbols in this **Air** card show how we can master our thoughts
to overcome conflicts and negative energy.

Amethyst is a powerful habit-breaking crystal. It wards
off psychic disturbance, brings peace, and helps us transmute
negative thoughts into healthy ones.

Rainbows inside crystals are said to be a sign of the
Shaman, who uses divination and metaphysical interactions
to bring about change. The rainbow's colors express positivity,
elevate our mood, and bring the victory of happiness.

Silver is symbolic of the moon and feminine ways. A silver
garment worn by a man represents the alchemical union of masculine
and feminine energies. The warrior in a **Silver Tunic** expresses a
state in which compassion, tolerance, grace, and optimism have
overcome anger, retribution, sarcasm, and pessimism.

REVERSED

If this card is upside-down in your spread, you may be stuck in
mental obsession. Ask the Universe to erase your "internal tape" of
anger, hurt, or disgust over others' behavior or inactions. Replace
the negative thoughts with an affirmation, such as, "I am a beautiful
child of the Universe, full of peace and generosity. I will not waste
the beauty of this day on another negative thought!"

For positive guidance, pull a new card. Contemplate the
elements of other cards in your spread.

CELEBRATION

Dance for joy!

Good times are finally here. Let go of your cares and have fun! Break out of isolation and join with others for a seriously good time. In Nature, a welcome rain after a long hot spell brings relief, giddiness, and exuberance. We are invigorated. We may need an occasion to end the "fun drought." Thank goodness for birthdays, reunions, and launches! A celebration re-energizes us and balances out long periods of labor. We all need more laughter, dance, and play in our lives, so live it up! It's the sunshine after the storm, the sparkling bubbly on a special occasion, and the fun free feeling of a Friday night after a long workweek. It is *your* turn to shine, to play, to dance!

Being with our community gives us a chance to eat, drink, and chat with cheer. The fizzy exuberance multiplies our happiness like bubbles rising to infinity. A great party is like a mini-vacation, whose joy lingers for days.

Don't be a stick in the mud or hold back because of self-consciousness. Grab the good times while you can! Delight like the children chasing around. Be present to times with friends and family and drink in the high points of life. Nothing lasts forever, so celebrate *now!*

ELEMENT: ▽ **WATER**   NUMBER: **11**   PHASE: **ENDING**

DEEPER INSIGHTS

Three friends from different cultures dance and play, riding bubbles of fun and happiness to infinity.

Celebration is the final card in **Water**, the element of emotions. Deep, communal joy is among the highest of all feelings and represents the completion of a spiritual journey.

Dance symbolizes the body overcome by joy. Music and dance are ancient expressions of goodness, gladness, and spiritual gratitude. The "waters" of our body dance together with others, like exuberant waves on a lake.

Spheres (or bubbles, in this card) represent wholeness and completion. The power of the world works in circles, such as each year coming around to mark an anniversary. The sphere is a three-dimensional circle: every point on the surface is equally distant from the center, just as the members of a community are equalized in an act of celebration.

REVERSED

We may resist truly celebrating with others, socializing only from a sense of obligation or duty. There can be no joy if we don't connect from our hearts with others.

If we are isolating, it may be a sign of workaholism or another addictive pattern, where we prefer to hide away.

Pull another card to see how you can break through the heart's obstacles, loosen up, and join the flow of fun.

CONNECTION

Cherish those who are
dear to you now.

Connection with our highest self often feels like romantic love. We each have an angelic self that deeply loves ourselves and others—when we allow ourselves to feel it. Maintaining this spiritual connection with our angelic self is the purest form of love we can experience.

If you're in a relationship, cherish your special one. If you're single, turn to your family, friends, and pets. Hold on tight to love in any form! Be consciously thankful for love's blessings, however imperfect others may be. When someone gives their heart in love, they become like an angel, carrying us through difficulties to better times.

To keep love close, guard against laziness or taking your partner for granted. Similarly, anger, jealousy, or insecurity can estrange our partners. If you stay kind to your love, together you can cross the difficult world ocean. If you feel emotionally distant or out of sync, make a "gratitude list" of all the best things about him or her. Recall how you met and how you felt about your partner then. Notice all the things, large and small, your partner does for you. Say, "Thank you for this love." Then turn the relationship over to the care of the Universe. Radiate your feelings of gratitude out to the community and see what...and whom...you attract!

DEEPER INSIGHTS

An angel carries his true love across life's arduous terrain.

The **World Ocean** represents the difficulties of our soul's journey in life. Our challenges can seem endless, as vast and relentless as treacheries at sea. Love is the Divine connection that guides us along our often harsh and lonely journey. If love is elusive on the human plane, try connecting with a pet or wild animal such as a songbird, fox, or squirrel. Through prayer and meditation, reconnect with your highest Self and feel the Divine love flowing to you from the angelic realm.

The **Angel** is our highest self, our direct connection to the Divine. Whether or not we have a human partner, each of us has the potential to connect with our inner Divine.

REVERSED

Sometimes our ability to be intimate is blocked. This card is in the **Water** element, so dark emotions such as shame, frustration, jealousy, fear, and anger may dam up our loving connection. Too much water overall can drown out our ability to be present with another, especially when we process deep or lingering emotions.

If you pulled this card upside-down, excessive stress, work, responsibilities, or plain over-scheduling may be draining you of the energy and time needed for loving connections. Check in with yourself to see what you have put higher on the list than *love*. Relationship is a two-way street: we need to give love *and* receive it. What is out of balance for you now? Pull another card for the answer.

CONTEMPLATION

Listen to the Universe
in silent meditation.

The difficulty you face can be helped by quiet meditation. Knowledge of our innermost self comes from deep contemplation. Our calling in life or the solution to a seemingly unsolvable problem emerges through inner stillness. Create or find a personal sanctuary in your home, workplace, or in Nature where you can sit undisturbed. Slow down your breath. Close your eyes or focus them on a single, fixed point like a candle. Enter into the present moment without distracting yourself. Unwind your mind's whirring thought-factory and simply Be.

If you are struggling with the Big Mysteries of life, try *saying less*. Listen more. Become aware of what you normally don't perceive. Don't speak every little thought that pops onto your tongue. Silence brings protection of all that we hold dear, especially those tender parts of us that feel most criticized, judged, or vulnerable.

If you are inspired with an embryonic idea, keep it to yourself and wait before brainstorming or sharing it with others. For now, contemplate a secret inner truth, just between you and the Universe.

ARTWORK:

"In Moments Hardly Seen Forgotten"

ELEMENT: ▽ **EARTH**   NUMBER: **4**   PHASE: **QUIETUDE**

A girl "bathes" herself in sage smoke.
Behind her, a pyramid appears in a Vision.

The **Pyramid** is a form of sacred geometry balancing between Earth and heaven, male and female. The pyramid's base is a masculine square shape. Each side of the pyramid is a feminine triangular shape. The pyramid's ancient mystery symbolizes human development, with its base facing in four directions and its apex facing heaven. Its symmetry is perfect, bridging between our world and the next. Of all the architectures on Earth, the pyramid remains standing after an earthquake. Our bodies take a pyramid shape when seated cross-legged in meditation.

The smoke from a **Sage Smudge** symbolically "washes off" the outside world, allowing us to enter a sacred space. Our consciousness enters the Divine Present, stilled and elevated beyond normal experience.

REVERSED

If this card appears upside-down, you may find it hard to get quiet time for inner work right now. The call to action may be too pressing, and you may resist being still. Though you know contemplation is important, other things feel more urgent. There is no action *per se* in contemplation. It is a time of waiting, gestating, and simply being. Yet it is as necessary to productivity as the fallow field is to the harvest. Silent introspection helps us incubate new energies and projects vital to our spiritual growth. Draw a new card to explore how to create quiet time.

CREATIVITY

Transform pure inspiration
into something concrete.
Make a creative mess!

Open yourself to the cosmic flow of energy. When we create, we convert inspiration into a form others can experience. Creativity can enhance any task from cooking to sewing, painting to singing, blogging to building a business. Being creative means we approach our idea without preconceptions. The creative process is messy and full of failed attempts. Art doesn't always "look good." Writers trash many drafts before finishing a novel. And filmmakers leave up to 90% on the cutting-room floor!

Put your Ego* aside and let Divine energy flow through you to others. Don't worry about how "good" it is. Focus on the *content* and the people your creation will serve. The environment is full of energies that don't have a voice or a face. Be like the artist whose job is to embody that energy, give it a face, and align it so it can reach people at the right time. All creativity is a process that involves trial and more trial, experiments, sketches, and tests. "Good enough" is good enough!

Don't be afraid of "bad" writing, a "lousy" drawing, or a botched recipe. Create! Play! Explore! And when you're done, then do it some more.   *EGO = **E**dging **G**od **O**ut

ARTWORK:

"Celestial River"

ELEMENT: △ FIRE   NUMBER: **10**   PHASE: **NOURISHMENT**

DEEPER INSIGHTS

The artist catches Divine inspiration in a golden bowl.
She transforms it into a play of colored light to glorify
the Universe and awaken others.

The **Golden Bowl** represents our talents and special gifts, which are a direct link to the Creator and creativity. We use these gifts to channel inspiration into creative works that nourish and inspire others.

The **Spiral** in rainbow colors represents the outward expansive movement of our creative acts. Like the spiral galaxy, our efforts spin out in widening circles to reach many others in time.

Gold is symbolic of the sun and masculine ways. A golden dress worn by a woman represents the alchemical union of masculine and feminine energies. The woman in a **Golden Dress** represents the outward manifestation of inspirations from the fleeting intuitive realm.

REVERSED

If this card is upside-down, you feel **Fire's** call to action, yet you're challenged to *make time* for creativity or *how to start* your project. Perfectionism may compel you to be too hard on yourself. Unrealistic expectations or low self-esteem remind us of the expression, "Comparing is despairing." Focusing on how "bad" your work is can be as egotistical as thinking you're the greatest ever. Keep your eye on your passion, and practice, practice, practice! Let go of the outcome and let the light of creative play in. Be messy. Have fun!

DESCENT

Step down from ways that
no longer support you.

No matter how high we've climbed in our career or worldly status, at some point we must descend. Great civilizations eventually fall. Growth reaches a peak and decline follows. Even the best of times come to an end.

Descent drops us into the "cave" of human experience. Loneliness and isolation crowd in. "Friends" from happier times vanish and we are abandoned to our lot. Yet treasures await us below if we accept our fall with positivity. We become more humble. Like the story of the Velveteen Rabbit, we become more "real." Many seek a spiritual focus after divorce, the death of a loved one, or a loss of fortune. Descent removes obstacles that separate us from the Great Mystery: it is like finding light at the bottom of a well, or discovering that beneath the lowest abyss lies the portal to Infinity.

Humble yourself to the Will of the Universe. Accept descent and be willing to learn the lessons of the current hardship. Loss helps us get to the bottom of things and see what lies beneath. After soaring the heights, we find that good old Earth feels pretty comfortable underfoot.

ARTWORK:

"Treasure Hunt"

ELEMENT: ▽ EARTH   NUMBER: 2   PHASE: DECLINE

A buccaneer descends into a cave, searching for buried fortune. A gold seam runs through the stone floor, but it can't easily be seen . . . or taken. The young man hopes for a treasure chest. Instead, once he adjusts to the darkness, he claims the entire mine!

The **Bat** is our metaphysical companion during descent. Bats "see" in the darkness and sleep upside-down. The bat represents the part of ourselves that safely and surely navigates our difficult circumstances.

The **Gold Mine** symbolizes the spiritual wealth that is ours when we understand that the hardest of life's experiences are often its greatest gifts. An accident can be a wake-up call that gives us a whole new approach to health and wellness—and a longer, happier life! Getting fired from a job may be the best thing that happens on the way to a new—and more suitable—career. The romantic breakup opens the possibility of a true soul mate coming into our life. Loss amplifies our gratitude for everything we have and all the lessons we have learned.

REVERSED

If this card appears upside-down, we may want a quick, easy fix. Impatience compels us to take dangerous or compulsive actions in an effort to stop the natural course of events. Denial of our situation can prolong the difficulties. If addictions are present, we may be at risk of a relapse or slip. Take a deep breath and pull three more cards for guidance on how to accept the changed circumstances of this descent.

DIRECTION

Slow down. Clarify.

Commit to a single path.

Oh, indecision! You are the bane of life's crossroads. The Air element can be dizzying, with multiple ideas and options scattering our attention, blowing our minds every which way. So many possibilities! Yet we can only do one thing at a time. Take a stand, make a decision, and stop spinning your wheels. Did you know that not deciding *is* a decision: it's choosing to stay where you are. Timing is important, but so is orienting yourself. You may think you can do twenty things at once, but you'll quickly exhaust and confuse yourself. And then where will you be?

Imagine there is no possible "wrong" choice, as long as we *commit* to a particular direction. The trials and errors along the way will lead to our destination—or steer us towards a different goal. We may want a shortcut, but bypassing a life lesson is just another way to get "lost." Take a deep breath. Pray for clarity. Then ask others how they found their way . . . and how they continue to find it. Everyone wanders about in a fog on occasion.

Do your best to contain your energy and stop running away from yourself. Get out of your head. Take aim. Then take action. Put one foot in front of the other and go!

ARTWORK:

"Whirlwheel"

ELEMENT: △ AIR   NUMBER: **2**   PHASE: **STASIS**

DEEPER INSIGHTS

A young woman spins at the crossroads of four directions and four elements: Earth, Air, Fire, and Water. The choices seem infinite. How can she know where her future lies?

This **Air** card speaks to the confusion of trying to figure out life in advance. Fear of making mistakes or taking a "wrong" turn can prevent us from trusting that we'll be guided in the direction of our soul's highest good. The **Wheel** spinning in mud represents enormous effort without forward movement. The **Map** symbolizes the theoretical or imagined courses we might take, without clearly indicating the "best" way to proceed. Only through forward movement can we know whether we're on track.

The antidote is to move out of the head and take *action*. Our own experiences give us all the guidance we need. We cannot *find* our way until we are *on our way!*

REVERSED

If this card appears inverted, we may not even realize we are at a fork in the road. We may simply feel stuck, as though we have no options and can't see the choices in front of us. Or we may not be paying attention to our course and instead bumbling aimlessly through the days.

Look at the other cards in your spread for different avenues to explore, or pull another two or three cards for inspiration.

DISCOVERY

Dig down. Uncover what's
been there all along.

How often do we trip over some ordinary thing, only to have it spontaneously take on deeper meaning? What you've been seeking is right underfoot, hiding in plain sight. Brush it off, consider it anew, and discover the original values and meanings that have been obscured.

Most of us take things for granted. Then one day we stumble over something normally overlooked. We have a serendipitous "Eureka!" moment that shifts our reality. A friend shares unexpected good news, we chance on a great new idea, or find a place we thought only existed in our imagination. Or . . . we learn that there's a skeleton in the closet, that we have an unknown half-sibling, it turns out we were adopted, or our employer is not who we thought. Discovering information can profoundly change our identity. We may become empowered, humbled, confused, or angered by what's come to light. Regardless which feelings are aroused, the facts are now in the open. We will never be the same. The challenge is to use new information for our growth.

Dig down through the layers to discover what awaits you. What have you been overlooking?

ARTWORK:

"Ancestral Ash"

<table>
<tr><td>ELEMENT: ▽ EARTH</td><td>NUMBER: 3</td><td>PHASE: GROWTH</td></tr>
</table>

DEEPER INSIGHTS

A girl meets her Great Grandfather's Spirit and discovers her forgotten heritage. The secrets of ancient writing, past civilizations, and fossils reveal her roots and awaken her sense of belonging: to Nature, and to a Nation. She begins to understand and accept her true self.

Petroglyphs symbolize a coded pictorial language we don't readily understand. They refer to the lost stories and facts of our ancestors' lives, a record to be deciphered.

Fossils connect us to all life forms on Earth. We're often focused on differences instead of similarities. We share much more with all others than is usually acknowledged, while our unique identity helps us find our "tribe" and their specific way to proceed in the world.

REVERSED

If this card appears upside-down, there may be resistance to us seeing and accepting the truth about our situation. The **Earth** element easily buries or mires important details. We may not have all the facts. The muck of half-truths and partial information may leave us stymied and uncertain, and we may be tempted to jump to conclusions. Instead, it may be wise to roll up our sleeves and dig more deeply into what is hidden.

The inverted card can also indicate a point in life where we want our identity to be firm and intact. We don't want or need to know more! Yet self-knowledge is an endless quest, and resistance to delving deeper only keeps us limited. Draw another card to uncover a fresh clue for your journey.

EMERGENCE

Break through
to the next level.

Life is a series of phases with occasional abrupt transitions. Like a giant staircase, we spend a long time in each stage before emerging into the next. Our bodies go through periods of growth, fertility, and maturity. Similarly, our *spiritual awareness* evolves in planes of understanding and awakening. We slowly integrate until unexpectedly one day, we find we've arrived at a new level.

You may feel like part of you has been in a cocoon or in hibernation "forever." Or you may feel you've been in a storm of chaos and difficulties without end. Either way, many elements need to be organized inside before we can emerge. The breakthrough means we are finally past the dormancy or blockage.

Awareness and intentionality help us bridge between the preparation stage and our emergence. Patience and endurance can help us stay in tune with the natural timing of our growth. Don't force or rush the process. Just let it unfold. Keep working steadily toward the goal. Trust that the veils will part and the Universe will reveal its secrets to you.

"Artemis Parting The Veil"

ELEMENT: △ **FIRE**　　　　　NUMBER: **9**　　　　　PHASE: **BEGINNING**

*The adolescent goddess Artemis parts the veil to peer at the inner workings of the Universe. The pregnant **Moon**, ruler of fertility, reveals her secrets to the fledgling goddess.*

An emergence is a one-way transition. It involves metaphysically peeling an outer skin to reveal something new. The **Phases of the Moon,** worn here as a crown, express the stages of disappearance and visibility that characterize emergence. In a single day, a girl disappears and there emerges in her place a woman with new powers, responsibilities, and risks. The last days of childhood are a kind of cocoon, to which there is no return.

This **Fire** card often shows up after a long period of dormancy, "treading water," or intense hard work. Graduation, promotion, and rites of passage like marriage, parenthood, and retirement are each an emergence to the next level of being. The "coming out" of a gay person or a debutante, the ribbon-cutting ceremony on a building, and the launch of a project emerge in new beginnings.

REVERSED

When this card is inverted, now is not the time to go public. Like breaking open a cocoon prematurely, the transitional stage inside is neither caterpillar nor butterfly, but indeterminate. More work needs to be done in the name of completion, protection, and preparation. The advice is to wait.

EXPANSION

Enlarge your
capacity.

Develop your small idea by going big. Expand! Add that addition, flow to the next phase, widen the circle. Stretch to make room and accommodate the new energy coming in. Open your heart to receive the love, the compliments, the inspiration that others are trying to give you now. Like the pregnant mother, allow yourself space to receive new life. Something special is coming through you now, so prepare to give birth.

At times we may already feel stretched to our limits. Yet expansion doesn't take something from us: it *gives us more* of what we need. A sole proprietorship grows with a new employee. A farmer acquires the adjoining land to work. A trip brings new horizons for you to explore. A family prepares for a brand-new member. Reassess your commitments and discard those that drain your energy. Delegate what you can to others. Extend your reach. And trust that the Universe will ripple open to meet you.

The mother asks her unborn child, "Where do I end, and you begin?" Similarly we can ask this same question when we work in service of the Universe.

ARTWORK:

"Where I End"

DEEPER INSIGHTS

The pregnant mother feels her baby move and speaks to it through touch. Her whole body expands in universal spiral patterns from the curled embryo, to her swollen breasts, to the whorls of hormones coursing through her body.

This **Water** card encourages us to open our hearts to limitless expansion, growth, and the absolute actualization of our dreams. The more we dwell in the feeling of abundance, the more bountifully our dreams manifest! If seeking prosperity, we can now free ourselves from all restrictions. Imagine there are no limits to our goal: money, time, and resources flow in endless abundance.

Metaphysically, the Expansion card concerns **Pregnancy**, whether literally adding to your family and bringing another soul to Planet Earth, or nurturing a business, project, or plan in its early stages. Let your heart feel the welcoming of new growth. Then remain open—and grateful—to how and when this wonderful event can transpire.

REVERSED

We may be restricting what is possible out of a fear of scarcity. Time, money, energy, and resources belong to the Universe. We may need to loosen up and stop trying to own and control how things proceed. For ideas on how to get into the flow of abundance, look for other **Earth** cards, or pull a new card for guidance.

FORGIVENESS

Let your heart be free.

Get ready to release the past. Old grudges dissolve with tears. When we shed resentment's dark clothing, only the essence of our interaction with others remains. Our purifying tears of forgiveness dissolve the stains of hatred and torment. We may feel deep emotions on our way to forgiveness. We cannot release our furious grip on others without experiencing and accepting our own rage, pain, disgust, and "ugly" feelings.

Sometimes the best path to forgiveness is to help others heal from similar trauma to what we've been through. By learning about *their* stories and the people who hurt *them*, we can glance peripherally at our own perpetrators, the way we look to the side of a star to see it more clearly. Forgiveness means to understand and to accept that even the worst people are humans—even though they act in ways that are deeply mistaken, addictive, or ignorant. Each us is capable of behaving badly. When we forgive ourselves for our transgressions, we become able to forgive others. When we see the larger picture and realize others have suffered as we have—or worse—we find compassion for them and ourselves. We gain insights into the people who perpetrate hurt on others. They transform from monsters back into human beings. Still, the hardest person to forgive may be our own self. It is time to let go, release, and forgive others—and ourselves. We can be free again!

ARTWORK:

"Wilderness Bath"

At the edge of the lake, a bather makes her final peace with the oppressor of her past. Her suffering and release flow into the cosmic waters. Forgiveness cleanses her.

One of the best ways to forgive another is to pray for him or her every day for at least fourteen days. If we pray for that person to have all the things we desire for ourselves: friends, love, success, happiness, health—and if we realize that they, like us, are learning about life and simply wanting the best—our hearts soften with forgiveness and we feel deep relief.

REVERSED

There is still work to be done before we can forgive. This card appears in the **Earth** element, because lack of forgiveness is stored in our bodies and can make us literally sick and vulnerable to disease. Forgiveness does not mean giving a perpetrator permission to continue abusive or unacceptable behavior. We still need healthy boundaries between ourselves and harmful people. Perpetrators of crimes still deserve proper punishment. We can be safe!

Check for cards in the **Water** element to see what might help you experience true forgiveness.

GENEROSITY

Share your riches freely and accept help from others.

"Pay it forward" and spread your wealth! Giving generously of your time, gifts, help in service, kind words, or human touch is a win-win exchange. Practicing philanthropy, being the "big sibling" to a young person, or helping a community recover from a disaster creates the inner glow of spiritual wellbeing. Nothing warms the heart like sharing your abundance with those in need!

Conversely, if you're down on your luck, allow others to give to *you.* Embrace the endless flow of material and spiritual help available. Accepting help restores our faith in humanity and helps us keep going—with hope.

Reflect on these questions: If you were on a horse, would you give a ride to one on foot? Or, if you were horseless, would you accept the ride? All material and spiritual wealth comes from the Universe—as does deprivation and lack of all kinds. There's nothing *fair* about who "has" and who "has not." We always have more of *something* than someone else, and less of another thing than someone. By giving and receiving, we equalize the distribution, and find we have everything we need.

Try this affirmation: "Help and abundance are everywhere. I open my arms to give—and receive."

DUALITY CARD

ARTWORK:

"Kindness Of The Heart"

ELEMENT: ▽ EARTH   NUMBER: 10   PHASE: NOURISHMENT

DEEPER INSIGHTS

Three wealthy ladies on horseback encounter a young waif in rags. She carries her possessions in a grimy blanket, has not eaten in days, has already walked miles, and smells of sweat. One of the noblewomen reaches down in kindness to offer her a ride.

Generosity is a **Duality Card**. *Giving* to others helps us feel in control. *Receiving* is more complex. The pink sky and green forest are two colors of the **heart**: unselfish love toward our fellows and the flow of vitality and community through their love to us.

Most of us are generous. We tithe, donate groceries, or give to charities. Giving warms the heart and reminds us to be grateful for our excess. It's a position of strength.

When we need help, we're generally weak, inexperienced, humbled. We may even feel shame or failure. Yet everyone needs a hand sometime. Can you accept the help offered unconditionally, from kindness?

The **Horses** are a key. A horse represents the earthly face of Godly power. The horse offers grace, freedom, and our "ride" to infinite possibilities. Its four legs take us to the four directions. Our nobility and productivity return.

REVERSED

We may be clenching on to what we have, not comprehending that others are asking for our time, financial support, or basic tolerance and acceptance. It's time to open our hearts and let **Earth's** bounty prevail.

If we are in need, our pride or shame may be edging out what others offer us now. Look to **Water** for advice.

GRACE

Let the Universe
support you.

Imagine wearing a dress made of stars, whose fabric is made from the cosmos. All the elements merge to make this Divine robe: **Air** from the swirling clouds, **Fire** from the galaxy's starry lights, **Water** flowing in ripples, and **Earth** represented by the beautiful woman's body. To wear such a dress, to be clothed in the splendor of Creation, is to be in a state of bliss that swirls and spirals outward to infinity. This is the *Grace of the Universe*, which lifts us up when we can't walk any further.

Grace restores self-esteem. We can all use help remembering to love ourselves. Sometimes negative thoughts, self-hatred, and shame get in the way. Other people bring us this grace purely and simply, without our need to manipulate or it figure out.

Like a celestial Cinderella, you can wear an attitude as beautiful as a cosmic dress. Know that you are a child of this Universe, as precious as any star in the heavens. Embrace your bliss, confident the Universe provides for your needs and clothes you in grace and spiritual beauty.

The Grace card reminds us that the Universe showers blessings on us. Grace can be obvious, such as good timing, a stranger's kindness, or being forgiven a transgression. Grace dwells in our natural talents and strengths, good health, or our spiritual awakening, which may come through hardship.

ELEMENT: △ FIRE   NUMBER: **8**   PHASE: **NOURISHMENT**

DEEPER INSIGHTS

A woman wears a Dress of Stars as she weds her Destiny.

We come from the **Stars** and return to them. While here on Earth, we're literally made of stardust. Our personal **Dress of Stars** is really our human body. Life is a precious gift. Grace is the birthright of each human being.

Stars guide our way in the darkness. For centuries, stars were the only reliable map for travellers by land or sea. The constellations point to immense forces affecting our born personalities and our daily experiences. We live inside a celestial clock, whose stars foretell events and influences for better or worse. To align with the stars is to act in accordance with the blessing of Divine Will.

REVERSED

The timing may be off. When the Grace card is upside-down, we are out of alignment with the Universe and its cosmic wheels of fortune. We may be trying to "push the river" or impose our will on a situation. Lingering insecurities, frustration, or deprivation may push away the Universe's gifts. The time calls for patience and faith.

Find something—anything—you're grateful for. Take a moment to feel a star seed of faith light your heart. Then take a deep breath, shuffle the deck, and pull two more cards: for spiritual and practical guidance.

HARVEST

Collect the bounty
you've earned.

It's payday! Our hard work has paid off. We have earned a great reward. We reap the fruit of our labor, prepare a feast, and rejoice in bounty. The luxuries of rest, celebration, and daydreams are ours. Enthusiastically, we imagine refinements and variations on our next success. Still, we are humbled knowing that the Universe **granted us** good timing and fertile conditions for the harvest. Hard work alone isn't enough. We need grace and luck, and a **plan** for our winnings so we don't waste them.

As we harvest, it's important not to distract ourselves with minor blemishes. Nothing is perfect, and thank goodness! Perfection is stagnant, brittle, and limiting. Instead, seek wholeness, a dynamic process in which the "win" is big enough to tolerate a few worms and bruises.

Invite others to help harvest. Later, everyone joins in the food, fun, and lightness. The time of wealth and celebration fills us for days and weeks to come. Like the farmer who saves a seed crop for next spring, we're careful to save as much as we can for the next "planting," knowing this time of bounty will also pass, as life's ups and downs circle on their merry-go-round.

ELEMENT: ▽ EARTH   NUMBER: **8**   PHASE: **ENDING**

A chef plucks a golden apple from a tree.
His windfall infuses him with awe and excitement.

Compliments, attention, and success are yours! The **Golden Apple** is a magic symbol of vitality and abundance that flows long into the future from the work you have done. Spiritually, the golden apple represents Divine food. Wisdom and knowledge, from worldly and other-worldly experience comes from this golden apple of the harvest.

The chef's **fork** implies a recipe or plan for the harvest. Look to the future to consider the best use of your harvest. The two tines of the fork mean there may be a choice or decision to consider. The fork also alerts us to guard our harvest from those who may envy us now.

REVERSED

The timing is off. Attempting to pull green fruit off the tree is exhausting, and impossible. Waiting until the fruit falls gives us an over-ripe, rotten harvest.

Our goal is blocked or out of reach. This isn't the best fit for us. Or perhaps we're trying too hard. We may exhaust ourselves, believing that we'll succeed if we work harder, smarter, faster. Though famine is part of Nature, we may be going against the Universe. Is this really the right direction for us now? What is the lesson if we look deeper?

Try a fresh Past-Present-Future spread for deeper insights on your situation.

IMMIGRATION

Walk in the
other person's shoes.

DUALITY CARD

Peace lies in accepting other human beings as they are. But how can we ever **understand** "the Other" . . . our enemies, political opponents, or foreign cultures?

The key lies in "immigration." When we cross over the cultural divide or "play on the other team," remarkable new insights are revealed. Our most intense feelings of disagreement about what is "right" and "wrong" stem from beliefs based on religion, politics, wealth, sexuality, or nationality. It's easy to whitewash anyone who thinks differently than we do. But sweeping generalizations are dangerous and limiting. Each unique person can be seen as a "country," with individual customs and ways. If we never expose ourselves to other "cultures," our ability to care about others is stunted. We lack understanding, unless we have tried in some way to experience the struggles they face. Compassion lies in awareness that all people belong to the same "human family" that we do.

Before you judge, learn what your enemies are **really** saying. Then transmute, cross over and see **yourself** from the enemy's viewpoint. What you learn may surprise you.

"Never judge a man until you've walked two moons in his moccasins." —Native American Wisdom

DEEPER INSIGHTS

A Cheyenne Warrior, forced off the land, survives on the fringes of the White Man's world. He meets other displaced people: descendants of slaves, political refugees, and those who resort to desperate acts to survive. Even while he works for a paycheck, his soul remains wild and free. Struggling in a changed world, the Brave's heart grows to respect that there is more than one way to live.

Each person goes through many stages in life. In this Duality card, **Time** is a key to having compassion. Old ways are outgrown and we no longer live as we once did. Immigration is like time travel: we become a guest in new reality. As times change, the principle of tolerance that underlies immigration, helps us remember we are guests in God's Universe at all times.

REVERSED

We resist seeing our own faults. Judgment closes our mind and we project onto others what we don't like about ourselves. If we could actually see inside another's reality, we might discover that they are far more like us than imaginable. This **Air** card calls us to look at our thoughts.

If you find yourself judging others, try turning the judgments back around and ask the same things of yourself. If someone seems lazy or thoughtless, ask where do laziness and thoughtlessness dwell inside YOU? We have the most to say about others, when those flaws are actually inside us. Pull another card, or look to the **Earth** cards in your spread to see how you can release judgment and find compassion and forgiveness for yourself—and others.

INITIATION

New powers are yours.

Wake to the mysterious workings of the Universe! A new beginning is at hand. You are about to be initiated into an important new stage of life.

The rite of passage, where we acquire new responsibilities, privileges, and powers, is one of the most profound transformations humans undergo. Leaving the harbor may be fraught with challenges. Part of us wants to cling to the old familiar life we had. We may feel inadequate or unprepared for a change and want things to stay as they have been. Yet the time has come and we can't delay embarking on the next expanse of our journey.

Your *feelings* will help you navigate this inauguration. Grief, anxiety, desire, and excitement are all natural emotions during a major life transition. Keep a journal to access your deeper thoughts, memories, and wishes. Make sure to spend time with close friends or family members who can witness your change and support you now.

Then welcome your new role as an Initiated One. Release yesterday and embrace your new power as you finish one of life's chapters and start the next. Like learning to puppy-paddle, test out your new powers one stroke at a time, knowing that with practice comes mastery.

ELEMENT: ▽ WATER   NUMBER: 4   PHASE: BEGINNING

DEEPER INSIGHTS

A teenaged Artemis stands beneath the crescent moon, empowered as a fledgling Goddess.

The Initiation card is all about wearing a new **Crown**. It is the promotion or new job you've been waiting for. Or becoming a parent or grandparent. Or, you've done the work and now cast off from familiar shores to a new sea of spiritual mastery. The crown denotes that you are the victorious ruler of your situation. It's a great time to review your deep values and reinforce your connection with the Divine. Metaphysically, the crown represents a halo, radiating your core virtues and moral conduct to those in your charge.

This **Water** card is ruled by the **Moon**. As the moon pulls the tides, so Initiation tows us toward new horizons. At times we feel in over our heads with unprecedented responsibility, at the dictates of a storm greater than ourselves. The moon's phases remind us that everything ebbs and flows. The time of turbulence will wane and we'll feel solid ground beneath our feet again.

REVERSED

The new opportunity on our plate is not going to come through in the way we hope or expect. But this may be good news, because it is not a true fit for us! The Universe has something better in mind.

INNOCENCE

Start again with
a clean slate.

Sometimes we need a completely fresh approach to life. By being inwardly still and pure, we open and become present to a new beginning. When we start a new job, take on major responsibilities in our family or community, or undergo a significant health change, we return to a state of innocence.

Like the baby, we need to lean on the strength of others. We may feel vulnerable, lost, or afraid when asking for help. But a new beginning is the proper time to seek guidance from a mentor and let others lead the way. Approach the situation like the baby: open, curious, and excited! We allow ourselves to be "parented" by those who can show us the ropes. They can support and watch over us as we find our footing.

Spiritually, once we are highly consciousness of the true nature of existence, a kind of "mature innocence" returns. The world feels indivisible and whole, as it was before we were born. We flow harmoniously with the universal rhythms and experience life energy as loving goodness and oneness. All things in the world look very different, and we see as though for the very first time.

ARTWORK:

"And The Stars Look Very Different Today"

ELEMENT: ▽ **WATER**   NUMBER: **5**   PHASE: **BEGINNING**

DEEPER INSIGHTS

The baby wobbles and 'stands' with his mother's help. He is utterly pure, with only the slightest knowledge of the world. He feels hunger, gurgles and cries, and falls asleep. All the rest of life is a wonder to him. As the baby explores, a record is made: the start of what will become recognition and memory. For today, there is only the Present.

There is no **Mother** without a **Baby**, and vice-versa. The Innocence card expresses a relationship with clear roles and attitudes. The mother is caring, patient, and protective. The baby is curious, receptive, and blameless. These roles and attitudes apply to variants of the mother-baby, such as teacher-student, master-apprentice, and expert-novice.

The **Sun** symbolizes the source of life as well as the self. As the baby contemplates the sun, he becomes aware of what he is and what is outside himself. The sun symbol refers to endless wonder at the mysteries of the Universe: the "Beginner's Mind" in Buddhism.

REVERSED

We resist letting others help us get started. Common culprits are a fear of not looking good/fear of vulnerability, or excessive pride. Or we may feel angry, confused, or jaded about learning something new.

To overcome these challenges, look at the other cards in your spread or pull a new card. Consider what the **Elements** are saying to you now.

INTEGRATION

Incorporate your childhood self
into today's adult.

Even after we've decided to change old behavior patterns, *change* takes determination, courage, and effort. Making a permanent change is like having a metaphysical makeover. We see in ourselves attitudes and actions that no longer fit. We say things we regret, in an unpleasant tone of voice. We don't speak up when we should, or say "yes" when we mean "no." If you've been a chameleon changing yourself to fit in or please other people, now is the time to show your true color!

We can't just *pretend* to change. That would be as superficial and impermanent as applying cosmetics. Real change involves integration of the various parts of ourselves. We reunite the split-off, wounded, childish parts of ourselves with our functioning, responsible, grown-up self of today. Mentally, we "marry" our fragmented pieces together into a True Self. We can *think* and *speak* our way into acting whole and mature. We no longer have to appear perfect to others. We can own it all! Our past choices and life experiences—for better or worse—are living parts of our whole self.

Start by "acting as if" you already are the new person you want to become. With commitment and practice, by putting each part of yourself in its place, you'll become a person you like . . . and love . . . a whole lot better.

ARTWORK:

"Metaphysical Makeover"

The Bride prepares for the wedding. Not only does she "put on" her best self for the occasion, she commits to deep changes in order to start a new life with her mate. This metaphysical makeover is an act of personal growth and awareness, replacing old patterns with new ones.

The hexagonal **Crystal** structure shows the integration of the different facets of herself into a cohesive whole.

Metaphysically, the **Lipstick** means changing the words we say in order to reinforce our new identity. In this **Air** card, words crystallize thoughts. We talk our way into new actions. Surrounding the lipstick is a **Spiral**. This sacred shape represents the path to our whole self. To integrate is to stir together the disparate parts, using a spiral motion where each revolution brings us to a higher level of ourselves.

REVERSED

We're having trouble fitting our pieces into a whole. We may cling to "all-or-nothing" black-and-white thinking. Integration means accepting shades of gray. Try replacing the word "or" with "and." Allow for contradiction and complexity, for some parts to be one way and others to be another *at the same time*.

Check out the other cards in your spread to see where or what the fracture might be.

INTUITION

Listen to that quiet
inner voice.

Our intuition is a direct channel to our Higher Self. Our hunches guide us toward our Destiny—what the Universe has in store for us. We have a gut feeling we can't explain, but just *know* is right. That small, inner voice we barely notice warns us to avoid shady characters and bad ideas, but also nudges us toward whom we can *trust* and what will be helpful for us. Our intuitions are correct so often, it's a wonder we don't listen *always!*

It's tempting to think others know better than we do or that our hunches are nonsense. Intuition bypasses reason and logic. It gives us direct knowledge without conscious thought processes. It's a very feminine trait in a reasoning, rational world—yet intuition is one of the highest forms of *spiritual intelligence.*

Besides intuition, our unconscious speaks to us through the secret, mystical language of dreams. Pay attention to your own dream symbols. Write down your dreams and let them guide you. Later, you'll be astonished how accurately they coaxed you about what was really going on. Let the quiet inner voice be your guide. Listen to your heart. It's whispering the truth.

ARTWORK:

"Dream Journal"

<table><tr><td>ELEMENT: ▽ WATER</td><td>NUMBER: 6</td><td>PHASE: QUIETUDE</td></tr></table>

DEEPER INSIGHTS

The sun is up, the dream already fades into the subconscious. Ancient symbols whisper their secret language, waiting to be decoded. The dreamer writes it down before the dream melts away. What does it mean? All day the dream affects her, haunts her with a hidden truth just out of conscious reach.

The dreamer is reflected in a metaphysical **Mirror**. Intuition gives us a glimpse of ourselves, outside of normal time, space, and reality. It is our sixth sense, the portal to an alternate realm where physical evidence and reason are irrelevant. Intuition is sensitive and subtle as **Water** to the smallest droplet on its surface.

All the **Colors** of the rainbow appear in this card. We each have a special color that activates and empowers our inner world. Intuition is like color—it's a feeling, a state of knowing that drenches us in truth, yet cannot be explained to ourselves or others. We just simply *know*.

REVERSED

We ignore our intuition out of fear. We may be overwhelmed and stressed, not knowing where to turn—even though intuition holds the key! Past trauma or rigid beliefs can drown out gut feelings about a situation. We fear a challenge from others if we speak our inner voice.

What impedes trust of what we *know* to be true? Do we want a different outcome?

Pull another card to see how you can remove what's blocking your connection to yourself—and the Universe.

JOURNEY
Travel to a new understanding
and a new way of being.

Let another land or culture transform you. A trip abroad deepens our understanding of life and develops our character. When we expose ourselves to unfamiliar lifestyles, eat exotic foods, or learn new etiquette, we broaden our knowledge of human life. We stretch beyond our comfort zone and discover new interests, explore our boundaries, and overcome limitations.

Simply going beyond our comfort zone is a journey! Lessons and revelations await us. Outside our own neighborhood, folks may be friendly or hostile, with traditions different from ones we know. By venturing beyond the familiar, we widen our sense of where we really live or work. We confirm or unsettle our feelings of belonging. We find hidden delights, along with potential dangers.

Challenge yourself to navigate and "survive alone" in strange territory. Take a Native-style walkabout or Vision Quest, in which you venture alone in the "wilderness," face your fears, and return home. You never know! Your new worldliness and wisdom may bring into your life the very people—or situation—you seek.

Your journey of transformation begins now!

ARTWORK:

"Walkabout"

ELEMENT: ▽ **EARTH**　　　　NUMBER: **1**　　　　PHASE: **BEGINNING**

A cowboy leaves the ranch and heads for unknown country. He takes his faithful companion. Their adventures change everything—and last a lifetime.

The first card in **Earth** is the "hero's call" to a quest. The **Dog** is our companion on the journey. A dog symbolizes the instinctive part of us that sniffs out a new friend and barks at danger. The dog is a great mediator with strangers, and each of us has part of us that acts as our "dog." It might be our hairstyle or dress, a tattoo or object we carry. On this journey, we each have something welcoming that invites people to stop and chat.

The **Globe** or **Map** symbolizes the oceans and borders we cross on our spiritual journey. We get a different result in life by trying something different. To prepare, head home using an unfamiliar route, eat a food you've never tried, or rearrange the furniture. Break normal patterns to open yourself to the Hero's journey.

REVERSED

We are stuck in an old, comfortable rut. The thought of change takes too much effort, or causes fear.

Or, the timing is off for travel. If we're planning a trip, it's wise to listen to our bodies and make sure we take extra steps to stay healthy, as adventure can stress sleep patterns and digestion. Money may be a limiting factor now.

Water and **Air** cards may have deeper information about the journey you intend. Check your spread or pull another card for guidance.

KNOWLEDGE

Expand your awareness and experience.

Further your education. Learn something new. Find a teacher, mentor, or online course and study a subject that engages your interest. Focus and concentration are like yoga for the intellect!

When we study what excites us, our enthusiasm for life surges. We become magnetic. We connect with a community who shares our interests, and we *shine.* One reward of concentrated learning is that we become more fascinating to others. Our conversational abilities expand. We're less mentally lazy, we remember details more easily, and people seek us out for our expertise and enthusiasm. A side benefit of following our passions and joining like-minded communities is that we greatly improve the odds of finding a mate. Knowledgeableness enhances our career prospects and helps us make lifelong friends.

Practical experience, such as an internship or apprenticeship is an essential component of learning. Without getting our hands dirty, classrooms, online exams, and theories only take us so far. Practising what we have learned makes it real. Take a class, join a group, and pursue your interests. Others of like mind will flock to you. You may soon have students—and admirers!

ARTWORK:

"The Wing Wherewith We Fly"

ELEMENT: △ AIR   NUMBER: 5   PHASE: GROWTH

DEEPER INSIGHTS

A girl reviews her vast knowledge. Language, geography, music, astronomy, astrology, literature, and codes all swirl around her head. Her formal education is a gift, not to be taken for granted. Life experience gives her immense depth. Many regard her with respect and awe.

This **Air** card explores **Language** as thought and knowledge. Math, music, maps, architecture, dance, poetry, astronomy, physics...Each realm of knowledge has its own language of symbols, rules, and structures. Becoming fluent involves theory and practice. Two planets guide the process.

Mercury is the planet of information and communication. Three times a year, Mercury's retrograde gives us the chance to review the conclusions we've made about life—review and if necessary, revise. Our minds begin as empty slates. As we grow, certain ideas get etched in. Mercury encourages us to rethink and revise our assumptions, conclusions, and attitudes—and keep reaching for more.

Opposing Mercury is **Saturn**, the taskmaster of hard work and discipline. Saturn constricts and confines, setting the limitations on time and human ability. *"Ignorance is the curse of God; knowledge is the wing wherewith we fly to heaven."* —William Shakespeare

REVERSED

We resist delving deeper into a subject we love.

If you have explored theory, try practice. If you've been doing practice for a long time, refresh or expand your knowledge base. Pull another card for confirmation.

LIBERATION

Break the chains of
old, limiting habits.

Break free from bondage: the old limitations in self-esteem, confidence, or optimism, that have held you back.

We can only stay limited for so long. At some point, we break out to a new level of freedom and scope. Our horizons open, restrictions fall away, and we are suddenly light with liberation. It doesn't happen by magic. We have to do our part. Without effort, we remain trapped in a prison of limitations. We must make important changes, reach for something better, and trust it can be ours.

Perhaps you've become very discouraged. Setbacks and problems seem to pile up on each other. Health problems beleaguer you. Limited circumstances hold you back from manifesting what you know is possible. Affirm to yourself, *"I am strong and successful. The Universe is bountiful. All that I need flows to me easily now from all directions."* Try it! Say it out loud. Then catch your next round of negative self-talk, and replace it with *affirmations.* Liberation comes from revolution, and moves from the inside out. Don't let doubt win. Fight back and break out to freedom. Yes you can!

ARTWORK:

"What's A Heaven For?"

DEEPER INSIGHTS

The stars align, allowing a man to break free of bondage. The chain snaps from his simple effort to liberate himself. Pluto is his oppressor; Charon, Pluto's largest of five moons, is his ball and chain.

Take a close look at this card. Everything you need to know about breaking free is there.

Try lifting your arms like the man in chains. How does it feel? Imagine grasping your dream in your hand. Visualize that dream connected to a distant star, whose powerful rays flow across the Universe to your fingers. Feel the chain snap and the ball fall away. You, too, can be free!

Pluto rules the Underworld. In mythology, its great moon **Charon** of Hades ferries souls across the river Styx to the world after death. These two celestial bodies symbolize oppression as well as a liberation. We each have a limited lifetime. Our choices lead us down to the underworld or up to heavenly realms. **Chains** represent our own limited beliefs and self-talk, often inherited from parents or society. To be our truest self means to individuate and break the links to past restrictive influences.

REVERSED

It's not yet time to break free. We wait for the Universe to align with our effort. We may be trying too hard. Or conversely, we may be depending too much on forces outside ourselves. Check in honestly about what's going on. Then, look to **Fire** and **Air** cards for the key to freedom.

PERSPECTIVE

Change your viewpoint.

Study the situation from a fresh angle. We may be locked into seeing only one aspect of what's going on. As adults, we easily get mired in our ways. The scars of traumatic experiences limit our perspectives and stunt our spiritual growth. "How important is it?" recalibrates our view and puts each challenge in its place.

Now, let's shift our point of view! If low, go high. If narrow, go wide. If looking inward, look outside, or vice versa. We reverse our angle to a new position that reveals what we've been missing. There is a whole spectrum in between squinting through a microscope and scoping out the wide panoramic view. Let's shake things up, recalculate our assumptions, and adjust our understanding.

Children live completely in the moment. They cry one minute and giggle the next. Because they know no bounds, they explore the world from every possible angle. They think nothing of rolling upside-down, climbing a tree, or running to the far end of the playground. The ladybug on a blade of grass is as fascinating as the shooting star. Free your mind to be like a child. View your current problem sideways. There is always more to it than meets the eye.

ARTWORK:

"What Meets The I"

DEEPER INSIGHTS

A boy somersaults every which way to get a better view of each and every thing in his world.

This **Fire** card shines light on our problem: a distorted viewpoint. The horizon in this card reveals a **Sphere**. This sacred geometry symbolizes wholeness, a rounded view of things, and the totality of possibilities. Though a **Fire** card, abstract mental qualities of **Air** can be seen in the analytic codes and graphics, reminding us of the spectrum between that which is serious versus silly or playful.

The contrasts in **Focus** are a metaphysical reminder about our attention. Limbering our focus through mental gymnastics helps us avoid habitual ruts of thought or perception. Instead, we keep a "Beginner's Mind" to our situation without preconceived ideas and limitations, the way a **Child** might.

REVERSED

We may be taking too much responsibility for the outcome of our situation. Fear, pessimism, and even sarcasm based on painful life experiences can creep in without our noticing. Or, we may simply be too close to the situation to have the perspective offered by time. Shuffle and pick another card from the deck for help with loosening up your view of things.

PRAYER

Tell the Universe
your dearest, secret wish.

When in doubt, go Up! Tell the Universe what's in your heart. Bow your head. Spin your prayer wheel or raise your arms to the winds of change. Trust that the Universe will hear you and respond.

Some people say that prayer is *talking* to the Universe and meditation is *listening.* A prayer from the heart is a humble request for help. When we pray for guidance, for others to be safe or healed, or for political peace, our yearning flows outward and is heard by the Universe.

The best prayer begins and ends with "Thank you!" In gratitude, our hearts radiate light and loving energy. We bask in cosmic wisdom and abundance. A simple prayer with or without words is enough. Laundry lists of names or "Dear Santa" wish lists of wants quickly turn into us *telling* the Universe what to do. When we stop bargaining with and beseeching the Universe, our awareness shifts from what we need or desire to the blessings we already *have.* As the saying goes, "Happiness is wanting what you have, not getting what you want." A pure and prayerful heart brings answers beyond our wildest hopes. And . . . whatever will be, will be.

ELEMENT: ▽ WATER	NUMBER: 3	PHASE: BEGINNING

DEEPER INSIGHTS

It is a mystery what happens during a prayer. A bride, focused and humble, sends her heartfelt wishes up to the Universe, and feels herself protected by light and strength.

This **Water** card connects our deepest heart and beliefs to the **Fire** of Divine Light. The **Rainbow** symbolizes the myriad possibilities that open through prayer. When we tune to the "prayer channel" our hearts open and connect with all beings, all situations, all solutions. Prayer is a miracle of human being.

A **Sphere** of protection encloses the praying bride. The sphere is sacred geometry, reminding us that our whole self is rounded and includes all parts: emotional, mental, physical, and spiritual. Prayer reconnects us with our totality of being.

REVERSED

Part of us is resisting prayer. Denial, laziness, skepticism, and busyness may be blocking our connection to the Divine. If we resist praying or don't believe it will help, let's get very quiet inside. Focusing on our breath, we inhale slowly and deeply. After a few minutes, the outside world falls away and we hear our heart beating steadily. We feel gratitude and wonder at how our heart beats during our entire life, and how it continues to beat until the end. We feel our problems float to the surface of our heart, exposed to the sky, dissolving in the celestial light of the sun, the moon, and the stars. Something shifts. That is the gift of prayer.

PURIFICATION

Find the light inside a difficulty.

It is time to transform poison into beauty. Toxic feelings of revenge, rage, and resentment are quite colorful, emotionally. Yet bright, colorful creatures in nature are often the most deadly poisonous. Similarly, left un-transformed, our intense negative feelings can make us quite literally sick.

The peacock teaches us a lesson in purification. The peacock's spectacular feathers come from what it eats, including toxic insects, frogs, and snakes. The peacock converts these poisons into bright, vivid plumage. Like the peacock, we transmute old harms and poisonous, obsessive thoughts into nourishment for our soul's growth. We morph the emotional darkness into spiritual light to avoid drowning in negativity.

Purification cleans the crud that clogs, pollutes, and dirties, to restore the pure original state of clarity, openness, and freshness. Think of clarified butter, or the treatment of waste water back into clear, drinkable water. It is only through compassion, conscious awareness, and doing inner work on our own dark tendencies that we salvage the treasures from our most difficult life experiences. We convert toxic rage into *spiritual victory.*

DEEPER INSIGHTS

The peacock transforms venom from the poisonous snake into glorious plumage. Wetland grasses filter impurities from water. A woman opens her compassionate heart to Planet Earth to heal the toxic atmosphere.

This **Fire** card is full of alchemical metaphors for psychological purification. The **Serpent** represents the poisons of base emotions like hatred, jealousy, and greed. The **Peacock** is our animal helper. This mystical bird is a sacred mediator between Heaven & Earth, ensuring that Light will vanquish the Darkness and that human sins or poisons will be absorbed and transformed into usefulness and spiritual beauty. The peacock further represents the midday sun. The eyes in peacock feathers are like the stars in the Universe, seeing all things and leading to a joyous and immortal afterlife.

Hard inner work, true maturity, and spiritual growth are the message here. Purification means we don't let ourselves off the hook. We hold ourselves over the fires of accountability and clean up toxic attitudes and behaviors. Through inner purification, we no longer tarnish the present moment with reactions of blame, self-pity, or disgust. Instead, we respond thoughtfully, kindly, calmly.

REVERSED

The resentment or emotional entrapment we experience may be more powerful than our willingness to dissolve it and move on. Check the elements of the other cards in the spread to see where to focus in order to grow spiritually.

QUICKENING

Everything comes together
and accelerates toward
completion.

At last, help is on its way!

There comes a point, after we've set our course and begun the hard work, when everything suddenly comes alive. Our undertaking gains momentum and things start coming together. This stage of growth is similar to the "quickening" in pregnancy when life suddenly enters the fetus. The baby starts to move and kick inside the mother.

No matter what we're trying to achieve, we always need a million things. Yet we each have only two hands and so much time and energy. Fortunately, the Universe "kicks in" at a certain point, and does for us what we simply cannot do for ourselves. Life enters and *quickens* our endeavors, or they will die. We bring our trust and faith to the situation. If what we started is "meant to be," all the puzzle pieces will fit together in time.

During a quickening, the pace builds up with animated excitement. Like adding fuel to a bonfire, we pay attention and *balance* the situation to keep things under control. We make sure to rest, pay the bills, and remember mundane details during the hectic quickening phase. Then, we enjoy the flood of new life energy!

ARTWORK:

"Come Together"

ELEMENT: △ FIRE   NUMBER: 7   PHASE: GROWTH

DEEPER INSIGHTS

A young woman holds her vision in her hands. Its rainbow colors surround her, while the missing pieces fly in of their own accord. Her vision quickens with life.

Fire activates this card in a process that resembles baking. The **Puzzle** pieces symbolize metaphysical ingredients in our recipe of manifestation. We gather all the pieces, follow the instructions, then let metaphysical fire do the rest!

The theme of reaching for the **Light**, begun in the **Liberation** card, now intensifies. The Universe's assistance takes various forms, from out-of-the-blue volunteers, to lucky timing, to circumstances finally shifting in our favor. We've done the hard work of committing to our dream, clearing out old baggage, and firing up the engines. Now the light grows brighter as the Universe opens to us, supporting our intentions and actualizing our dreams.

REVERSED

Obstacles prevent us from realizing our dream, despite our sincere intentions. The timing isn't right. Wavering faith makes our efforts inconsistent. We may be trying to do too much, or overworking due to perfectionism rather than welcoming help from the Universe. We're not concentrating on our vision, just hoping it will manifest "magically" by itself. Look to the elements in your spread to see which forces can energize and activate your goal.

ARTWORK:

"Those Sheltering Arms"

REBIRTH

Wake up to a new start.

We return to new life after a period of loss and numbness. What was dormant now awakens.

Our heart was broken. We suffered a loss. Daily stress overwhelmed us, and we shut down emotionally. It felt like part of us died. The pain, pressure, and chaos was too great, so we buried our feelings. We gave up hope, daydreamed aimlessly, or stumbled in despair. Until now.

Time heals all wounds. Spring always returns. The emotional "winter" felt unbearable, long, and harsh. Not everything will survive. We may be unable to awaken old dreams or resume abandoned relationships. Some projects are lost. Friendships neglected too long may perish. But we can thaw out our *feelings* and start again.

We redo our online profile, change our style, take another photo, and begin dating or job hunting again. For some people, a vacation or retirement brings much-needed rejuvenation and a second chance at life. We have changed, and so has the world. It's time to live again!

Life can and will be different than before. We all need renewal, a fresh start, and a chance to come back again after a long difficult season. We are reborn.

DEEPER INSIGHTS

A woman rakes away old leaves and unearths herself reawakening after a long, dormant stretch. Sparks of new life are in the air, and already the fields are green.

Rebirth is the last card in **Fire**. It is related to, but different from **Emergence** and **Resurrection**. All three cards concern new beginnings. While Emergence means *breakthrough* and Resurrection means *restoration*, Rebirth means *starting over again* after a symbolic "death." Here, fire has a warming, thawing, rekindling effect.

Roots sunk deep into the earth kept the old tree alive all winter. Our roots are our ancestry, spiritual beliefs, and our true calling in life. Like sheltering arms, these roots hold us until we're ready to rejuvenate.

The **Rake** metaphysically untangles past issues that caused the "death." This death can be literal or symbolic. After a cut-off or shut-down, Rebirth is a series of transitions. Gradually we gather strength, identity, and inspiration. The rainbow hues and magic stars surrounding the awakening woman indicate unlimited opportunities. We give ourselves time to muse while re-awakening.

REVERSED

We may be grieving still. Grief takes many forms and includes anger, apathy, and numbness in addition to sorrow. Grief is a natural process with its own timing and stages. Reflect upon what, who, or which aspect of yourself may have died. Shuffle the deck and intentionally draw another card for guidance. **Fire** and **Water** cards are particularly helpful.

RECEPTIVITY

Tune in - with care - to the
Universe's guiding rhythms.

Empaths feel everything and everyone. Life sometimes feels so complex and overwhelming, it's hard to focus on ourselves! Listen to the music of life: at every moment, we're awash in energy currents of colorful light, radio waves, and frequencies beyond perception. There's social media, advertisements, mail. Everyone around us is going through difficulties, dramas, and dilemmas. There's so much *noise* out there, it's hard to decipher what is truly helpful. No wonder we sometimes seem preoccupied with—or grasping for—our own ideas and beliefs: they represent a small island of "sanity."

Opening ourselves to new influences can be hard. Yet if we close off from outside input, we'll only get more of what we already have—our own "best thinking"! People tell us repeatedly what we need to hear, but often we don't, won't, or can't listen. Receptivity means having the awareness and willingness to selectively absorb messages from others, taking what we like and editing out what doesn't fit.

When we're vulnerable to other people's moods, a clear sound can "reset" our nerves. A tuning fork or bell helps us align, dispel chaotic energy, and stay receptive to what's *useful.* Our breathing, heartbeat, and blood coursing through our ears is the original "music" that helps us tune into larger cosmic rhythms. Making time for natural sacred music helps us stay receptive to Source, while receptivity to fresh ideas helps us grow.

ARTWORK:

"Where My Heart Wants to Go"

ELEMENT: △ AIR   NUMBER: 3   PHASE: **REFINEMENT**

A woman strikes a Tibetan singing bowl. Its pure sound swirls in a vortex, entering her heart, re-attuning her to her inner Self and overcoming the interference from her deep empathy to others.

This **Air** card helps us understand the workings of our mind. **Spirals** are a sacred geometry based on a circle whose size or position changes with each revolution. Our thoughts can swirl themselves into a hurricane, or down to a tiny silence. The choice depends on allowing them to torment us or deciding to tame them through meditation.

Listening is a key to Receptivity. Metaphysically, to listen means to filter out the noise and let in the music. Musicians perceive sacred rhythms of nature, from crickets to thunderstorms. Tuning into these natural sounds inspires composition and performance. By listening quietly, we, too, can discern what's beautiful, important, and vital to us.

REVERSED

Our original idea still seems like the only valid choice. We can ask, "How is that idea working out for me today?" We may need to focus on Heart, Body, or Spirit, before opening our minds to new inspiration. The elements align with our being: **Fire=Spirit, Earth=Body, Water=Heart.** This card is in **Air=Mind**.

RECYCLE

Unravel your 'failures'
to build a new foundation.

Life is a patchwork quilt made from remnants of our past. All things are made of the basic elements of life. Nothing is permanent. The Universe recycles and so must we. The wreckage of our past has many useful pieces!

We all have limitations: a fixed number of days on Earth, only so much time and energy, our distinct strengths and weaknesses. Yet how much energy we waste each day! Regret, revenge, and remorse are thieves of emotional health. We rehash the same scenes over and over, unable to digest them. "Emotional entropy" devours our vigor, drains our soul, and squanders life on useless ruminations. We need to re-frame the past, to salvage the patches of good from the trash. A relationship or job ends, and we can't move on until we recount its lessons and incorporate them into our "revised" patchwork selves.

Lingering over the past is "emotional hoarding." We clean house and return to the present. We earn life's lessons with our own time and effort. We might as well take a "pay cut" in life if we don't reclaim ALL of ourselves. Each piece has indestructible meaning and worthiness!

Recycling means total self-acceptance. It's about loving every little inch of our lives, even the nasty bits.

DEEPER INSIGHTS

Mother Earth crochets our planet's rich resources from the four elements: Fire, Air, Earth, and Water. A woman rests, knowing she is cared for by the plentiful patchwork fields. The fragile atmosphere soothes her skin and lungs and gives life.
She lets go of all anger and pain.

This **Earth** card shows that Mother Earth rejects nothing. Her giant hands incorporate and rework garbage, bones, and ashes. The **Patchwork** blanket embodies a spiritual theme where **Love** is the thread that makes a most beautiful garment from scraps. People who joke about their foibles win our hearts far more than people who try to act "perfect." Self-love means laughing at a past that used to mortify us. We come back down to Earth and humbly accept our humanness.

The golden koi is our animal helper in the form of a **Fish**. Metaphysically, the fish means good fortune through abundance, luck, food, and longevity. The koi is sometimes thought of as a dragon of transformation, whose courage and perseverance brings renewal.

REVERSED

We may be feeling very fatigued despite doing "all the right things" like proper diet and exercise. When we're not ready to "own" everything in our past, we can feel drained and listless without knowing why. Pull another card or look to the other cards in your spread for the key to unlocking your self-acceptance.

REFLECTION

See yourself for
who you truly are.

There is a dark, shadowy side to each of us. We all make bad decisions, think destructive thoughts on occasion, and ultimately have to face our own mortality. There's so much about ourselves we don't want to see.

Let's look in the metaphysical mirror. Take a true look at our whole selves. We come out of denial and admit what is really going on inside. Breathe into what's not pretty, what we don't want to own, along with what we *like* about ourselves. We let ourselves be "perfectly imperfect" human beings! Carl Jung said, "There can be no transforming of darkness into light and of apathy into movement without emotion." It takes immense courage, humility, and feeling to admit, "I am willing to own my part in life. I have flaws and failings—and—I have the right to happiness, too! I have the right to be ME." Can we admit the truth?

No matter where we came from, what we have or have not done, it is time to face up to it and own it. We are all children of the same Universe. We all have access to grace, forgiveness, and hope . . . if we dare to face our truth and join the human species!

ARTWORK:

"Who Looks Inside Awakes"

DEEPER INSIGHTS

A woman studies herself in the mirror. She fights a battle that can destroy herself and her family. She has already lost many things, even parts of her own life. She faces her truth with courage and clarity. Her heart connects to eternity, the infinite unfolding splendor of the cosmos. She is clear about what she needs to do.

This **Fire** card shines light on our inner darkness. Most of us have distorted images of ourselves. We see ourselves as better or worse than we actually are. If our self-image is unbalanced, we tend to see others as better or worse than we are. This kind of "vertical" evaluation means that one person always has to be "good," while another is "bad." Here, the metaphysical **Mirror** reflects a new degree of self-honesty that is humble, leveling, and truthful. We own up to the less likable parts of ourselves while equally claiming our inner goodness.

Stars are a form of **Fire** that connect us to infinity and the Universe. Honest reflection means seeing that everyone—starting with us—has both light and darkness . . . which means that we're all equal in this cosmos!

Reflection echoes the spiritual processes in the **Forgiveness, Immigration,** and **Stuck** cards.

REVERSED

Our bias for or against ourself is preventing us from resolving the situation in question. Check the other cards or pull a new one to learn how to become willing to have a more realistic view.

RENOVATION

Burn away the old to
make way for the new.

Before planting a new crop, farmers burn their fields to clear weeds and residue, and prepare for new growth. Similarly, before we build something new, we must destroy what's deteriorated. Renovation depends on clearing out the wreckage. First we take stock to see what, if anything, is worth saving. Then we demolish and throw out the junk. The process of dismantling and rearranging can exhaust us . . . unless we bring a playful humor to it!

A forest after a fire looks desolate, though some trees *depend on heat* to open their cones. A hardship such as a failed business, an accident we didn't cause, or a painful divorce feels like we got "burned." Yet once we come out the other side, new "seeds" open for us that *needed* our dire circumstances! The bankrupt entrepreneur changes tactics and succeeds. The injured pedestrian discovers the rejuvenating powers of yoga. The single parent finds a more appropriate mate. Our values transform. We are free and clear to rebuild our lives in new directions. We change and adapt, renovating our livelihood, our physical fitness, our ability to love. We renovate our joy in *Life!*

ELEMENT: △ FIRE   NUMBER: 1   PHASE: ENDING

DEEPER INSIGHTS

A sprite playfully tosses fire into the sky as she skips over ruins. Though her task involves "heavy lifting" to clear out the rubble, she enjoys herself in fun. Fiery Mars, ruler of war and destruction, looks on from the sky.

Renovation is the first card in **Fire**. Before the new can be built, the old is destroyed. Cleaning up wreckage is dirty work, but that doesn't mean it can't be fun!

The **Circle Dance** is the oldest form of dance, the "dance" of stars in our spiral galaxy. This sacred geometry applies to the scouring or cleansing motion we need to make renovations. Going around and around clears up the details and lets us revisit our priorities. Sorting into basic groups like Save, Give, Sell, and Trash helps us dance quickly through the mess.

The planet **Mars** energizes our renovation. Its gift of determined action leads to conquest over old wreckage.

REVERSED

Anger overrules our potential to be light-hearted now. Rage + destruction = important things get ruined. By waiting, we avoid accidents we'll regret later. Direct the anger elsewhere, or ask for help. Remember the circle dance! Circular motion dissipates anger and includes others.

TIP The chart on page 148 shows the Divine Order of the cards. Find this card and others in your spread to see where you've been and where you're going.

RESOLUTION

Revisit the past and
resolve unfinished business.

Now we return home, revisit a former time, and reunite with our earlier self to settle old accounts. It's time to express words left unsaid, show feelings we hid, and ask questions that were never answered. We let the person we are today bring wisdom to help the person we were "back then." Together, the two parts called "me" and "Myself" can heal an old injury.

Perhaps we ran away, froze our feelings, or buried ourselves in addictive behavior to escape a painful childhood. It's never too late to resolve the past.

Maybe we need to clear up old family quarrels, rectify a wrong we did, or face a lingering misunderstanding with new maturity. It's often hardest to practice changed behavior around those who have known us our whole life. Our slowest-healing wounds come from those closest to us, in family, in our spiritual community, or at work.

We may face a tremendous amount of healing and recovery work to clear old scars. Yet time and the Universe—and a grateful attitude—help us confront the past, and restore harmony and ***wholeness***.

ARTWORK:

"Long Drawn Afternoon"

ELEMENT: ▽ **WATER**   NUMBER: **10**   PHASE: **ENDING**

DEEPER INSIGHTS

A young girl hugs her father's gigantic leg.
The family homestead sits in memory's golden afternoon.
Balance is restored and the inner work is complete.

This **Water** card swells with a powerful call to action. It takes courage to clean up the past. Not everyone can do it, but we've drawn this card so we must have the right stuff!

The **Giant** symbolizes the power of a parent or adult over a child. The adult figures in our lives may have protected and supported us as weak and vulnerable children. Or, there may be a perpetrator of abuse whom we now confront. The Giant expresses the degree of influence, consequence, and effect upon our lives.

Keeping ourselves safe is the highest concern in some resolutions. We may write a letter we don't actually send, but instead put in a "God Box" and let the Universe carry the message—similar to a "message in a bottle" on the sea. Whatever we do, relief and completion come through facing our past now.

REVERSED

It may not be the ideal time to confront the people, places, and things of our past. If we force a confrontation, it may backfire. Better to wait. Look more deeply at the imagery in your spread, or set an intention to find the missing details in a new card.

REST

Loosen your grip and
let yourself relax.

It's time to rest, to chill out, to let go completely. We let ourselves go dormant like a perennial in winter. We stop worrying and trying to figure it all out. Instead, let's visualize a peaceful image: lying on a beautiful beach listening to waves, or resting on a bed of soft clouds somewhere over the rainbow. Let ourselves feel "on vacation," in the most relaxing environment we know. Then forget everything …

Sink down, down, down into a state of **deep peace.** If we have trouble sleeping, we slow down our breath like a baby's and breathe from our belly. We affirm, "All is well! Tomorrow is another day. Everything will work itself out." Even during sleep, part of ourselves remains watchful. Solutions to problems often come during the state between waking and sleep, when we are most fully relaxed. A deep massage, a real vacation, or simply doing nothing for a day can open us to this resting but watchful problem-solver.

Even a few minutes repose in a state of cool stillness, brings rest and rejuvenation. Calmness clears the stains of the day. We drop our cares and troubles, knowing with confidence that the fallow field yields the best harvest.

ELEMENT: ▽ EARTH   NUMBER: **5**   PHASE: **QUIETUDE**

A girl sleeps like Earth in winter,
while part of her remains alert and watchful.

This **Earth** card reminds us of the deep stillness and inactivity of winter. **Ice** cools down our energy and stops all motion. We sleep late in the morning or retire early at night. We refuse to burn our candle at both ends. A break in our daily routine protects the quality of our health, work, and relationships.

This card explores the metaphysical aspects of the self at rest. The top figure rests simply and literally, while the bottom figure is unconscious, cased in ice. Between these two is a third figure, alert and attending the messages in our dreams. These three aspects of consciousness give us permission to relax and resume our tasks later . . . much later!

REVERSED

We've been overdoing it. We're resisting a break from work and chores. Deep down, we're driven by fear. Insomnia stalks us. We're trying to get enough rest and sleep, but our mind and body are not cooperating. If medicine or herbs aren't working, try regular *meditation*: slow down the breath and keep the eyes perfectly still, even when closed. A small ritual helps. Find a time of day that works consistently, then light a candle or incense, or play sacred music to support our practice.

Turn to the **Air, Fire,** and **Water** cards in your spread for insights on what's preventing your rest.

DUALITY CARD

RESURRECTION

Bring an old idea
 back up to the surface.

Bring an old passion back to life! Take that shelved "someday . . ." project out and dust it off. Regretfully, in the everyday rush of life we sometimes have to put aside things or people that are important to us. Responsibilities press down on us. Free time dwindles. We tell ourselves we'll put that special project on the back burner, take a "time out" from a relationship, or tone things down with a community. We'll re-prioritize, until our time and energy become free. Meanwhile, the things or people we've left behind haunt us with unfinished possibilities . . .

Without the hobbies, pursuits, and friendships that inspire us with passion, we remain spiritually empty and unfulfilled. If we can't follow our hearts, we become needy and vulnerable, acting out our worst behaviors.

Take that special project out of storage, reach out to an old friend, or reconnect with a favorite community. Delve into the hobby you always dreamed of doing. Resurrect the idea or relationship that was temporarily "submerged." We return to the place and the people that inspire us and let ourselves live again!

ARTWORK:

"As Sure As The Wind"

ELEMENT: ▽ **WATER**　　　　NUMBER: **7**　　　　PHASE: **BEGINNING**

DEEPER INSIGHTS

The fisherman squats at water's edge. His line is cast and he waits. In the mystical realm below consciousness, two mermaids pull in opposite directions at his dream. They play tug-of-war with the man's vision. Will he capture his dream? Or will it escape?

This **Duality** card is in **Water**. The resurrection can go either way, depending on the time. Either we hook the fish or it swims away. The **Mermaid** is part woman, part fish, symbolizing an incompletion. One mermaid holds our **Past** defeats and frustrations. The other expresses our hopes for **Future** fulfillment.

We're conflicted. Should we revisit this situation—or not? It didn't work before . . . what is different now? The guidance is to test it out. Push the "play" button and see where this situation wants to go and how it fits into our current life. We may have to give this resurrection three chances before we know for sure. If we're not able to put our heart into it, we can retire it permanently.

REVERSED

We want to get back to our important project or rekindle a flagging relationship, but now is not the right time. Other lessons await. Don't worry! We'll get another chance later. Other cards in our spread show us the priority, or we can intentionally pull a new card for guidance.

DUALITY CARD

REVERSAL

Make a U-turn.
Assess what you have
lost . . . and gained.

Sudden, unexpected change results in a reversal of fortune. Our expectations are over-turned. A new force unbalances the whole equation. Positive, light, expansive energy reaches its extreme and turns abruptly negative, dark, and implosive. Or vice-versa: a stroke of good luck opens an unanticipated opportunity. Unemployment, divorce, and bankruptcy are typical reversals. A sudden windfall such as a tax dividend, unplanned inheritance, an unpredictable but delightful encounter, or a mysterious surge in sales puts us on the upswing.

Reversals are life's U-turns. We head in a particular direction and abruptly change course. Relationships unexpectedly end or begin. We abandon the old course and shift focus.

During a sudden loss—or gain—contemplate what the Universe has taken from you . . . and what you still possess. Reversals reveal what is important in life, and remind us that *we are not in control!* The Universe laughs at our plans and doles out earthquakes or bumper crops with equal indifference. Being humble never hurts. "Owning" whatever we get helps us cope with our loss . . . or gain!

ARTWORK:

"Yin-Yang"

ELEMENT: △ AIR   NUMBER: **11**   PHASE: **ENDING**

Icarus flies towards the sun, falls from the sky, and hangs in limbo, clinging onto a thread of what he had before. The Yogi practices both upright and inverted postures, preparing himself for all situations. By remaining strong and flexible, he survives and thrives.

Reversal, the last card in **Air** is a **Duality** card. The situation can go either way. Once the extreme is reached, the only way forward is an about-face. Like a metaphysical sailboat, we tack back and forth to proceed against the winds of change.

Both figures **Hang** in mid-air. During a reversal, the ground can feel ripped out from under our feet. A **Solar Eclipse** turns day into night and flips our aspirations upside-down. The planet **Uranus**, ruler of unpredictable events, is at work. Uranus causes chaos, cosmic surprises, and sudden release. We find comfort in knowing that reversals are essential to preserve balance over time.

The **Yin-yang** backdrop made from a confusion of elements symbolizes our turmoil. **Fire, Water,** and **Air** scramble roles and affect the **Earth** of our bodies.

REVERSED

The reversal liberates us at first. But beware! The far-reaching consequences will affect us and pose challenges we hadn't anticipated. We're at the end of a phase where we operated under a certain set of ideas and values. With all overturned we reconsider how to navigate forward.

SEPARATION

Let go of what—and who—no longer works in your life.

DUALITY CARD

As day vanishes inevitably into night, so we retire failed projects, relationships that no longer serve us, and deluded old dreams that prevent our progress. We detach and distance ourselves from lingering hopes and illusions. It's time to say goodbye to someone or something we've held close. With neutrality and maturity, we drop our fantasies about life and grow up a notch.

Beware of trying to "stay friends" after the break-up, or chasing after someone who rejected us. When a sapling breaks, it's a messy fracture with dozens of pieces still clinging together . . . technically, the tree is "broken," yet it's still in one piece! A clean break preserves our self-esteem and shortens the recovery. Grief, necessary after a loss, can't start until we get off the merry-go-round of hope and despair that comes with "hanging on" and trying to fix what's clearly over.

Retire a worn-out ideal. A mini "funeral" helps us get over this ending. We go our separate way and lay this situation to rest. Our energy is freed to prepare for something new . . . and better!

ARTWORK:

"Even The Stars They Burn"

ELEMENT: ▽ **EARTH**   NUMBER: **11**   PHASE: **ENDING**

DEEPER INSIGHTS

The Queen of Night draws a cloak of darkness over the Earth, putting the day to rest.

The last **Earth** card, Separation is a **Duality** card. Between **Day and Night**, a landscape changes profoundly. A city view transforms from a beautiful park overlooking the harbor to a carnival of lights at night. It's like two different cities. Similarly, when we separate from a worn-out situation, we become unrecognizable from who we were before. Holding on—the other choice—leaves us largely unchanged. We miss the chance to transform. Instead, we repeat the pattern until we get the lesson.

Everything comes from and returns to Earth. Separation sometimes leads to an ultimate reunion—on new terms. The **Clouds** symbolize the nebulosity of holding on, the duality of assets and deficits to sort through as we separate.

The **Dying Star** symbolizes finality. We let ourselves grieve. The grieving process is like riding a wild pony—we just have to hold on and experience the feelings of anger, sorrow, and fear until it passes.

REVERSED

We're having trouble letting go. Denial and resistance won't prevent the inevitable. It's time for acceptance. To see how to navigate, draw another card or look at the other cards in your spread.

SIMPLICITY

Eliminate the excess.

Boil things down to their essence. In order to move forward, we have to let go of our baggage: material baggage, such as our possessions and the work it takes to keep them; emotional baggage, such as an old hurt or resentment and bitterness; and mental baggage, such as ideas about life and spirituality that don't ring true. We drop the rock, dump the baggage, release what has been holding us back, and simplify.

When we lighten our load, we pass through a narrow gate that leads to our Higher Self. This gate is one of humility, honesty with ourselves, and simplicity of being. The narrow gate is one-way: once we enter it, we can't go back to our former way of life and its limited understanding of what is truly important. We come to this earth naked, with no possessions. Similarly, we leave everything behind when our souls depart. Each letting go, whether material, philosophical, or emotional prepares us for our final destination. Our spiritual purpose is fulfilled not by outer acquisitions or beating the competition, but by simply releasing whatever has been holding us back and moving closer to our purest state of being.

Simplify, reduce, and move forward with ease.

ARTWORK:

"The Narrow Gate"

DEEPER INSIGHTS

A woman sheds her heavy coat and drops her burdens.
Free, she passes through a mystical gate and transforms
into a higher angelic state of being.

This **Earth** card underscores the transitory nature of our earth-walk and our relationship to worldly things. The **Urn** has multiple meanings. It symbolizes our body, the soul's container during life. An urn holds ashes of our ancestors, a metaphor for the expectations and beliefs our family imposed upon us. An urn of water signifies the heart and its emotions. The interpretation is open.

The **Letters** represent our responsibilities and legal obligations, the records of finances, property, health, and tax. The **Clothing** symbolizes the roles we play and the way others see us, our standing in society.

This piece honors all who had to shed our entire past, who lost our way, our job, our home, or our station in life. It is for anyone who has lost courage, direction, or the will to go on. The prayer is that we find the portal to true life and pass through to the other side.

REVERSED

We hold onto excess weight, clutter, or stale feelings. We cling on, mistakenly attaching our identity to outer conditioning and material things. Set an intention for a new approach and ask the oracle again.

STRATEGY

Brainstorm.

Then set your course

and go!

DUALITY CARD

Great achievements start with a plan. We sketch out the possibilities to find an optimal solution. To plan is to use the mind for its intended purpose: the organization of abstract information into an intentional pattern or blueprint. We manifest when we harness the mind towards accomplishment and away from worry and daydreams, the fuel of procrastination. Start by *visualizing* the end goal. Sketch it out on a dinner napkin. A feature film starts with a script. Check out how others have accomplished what we yearn for, the steps they took, the structures they used. Then plan something similar to get results like theirs.

Hard decisions are part of life. We plot our course and advance, or else we'll be stonewalled. It's tough and potentially dangerous to scale a major roadblock on whim alone. Strategic thinking, logic, research, and a game plan preserve our resources and indicate when to retreat. We persevere and re-chart our path as circumstances change.

Planning is a great way to overcome procrastinating and find a way over life's complex hurdles. We use prudence and caution, but don't delay. A good strategy, combined with resourcefulness, improvisation, and execution, overcomes all obstacles.

DEEPER INSIGHTS

The chess players are equally matched. Each man struggles to overpower the other with opposite forces of Fire and Water. Strategic thinking and a carefully decided action offer the only way out.

This **Duality** card in **Air** shows the elements in conflict. **Fire** and **Water** clash in a game of chess. The energy of Fire moves up, while Water moves down. We may need two plans: one for advance, another for retreat. There is more than one way to tackle the situation and achieve our goal. **Air** is the most flexible of all elements, and the only one that interacts to increase the potency of water into a hurricane, flame into a raging wildfire, or earth into a dust storm. Harness the power of the mind to make an abstract plan and think things through to their consequences before acting. Emotion has no place in business.

REVERSED

We're trying to navigate by *feeling* or *acting* before *thinking* things through. Hunches are helpful, but not enough now. Face facts and figures. We'll find our solution in research, planning, details, and rigor.

Some say, "God is in the details," so let's work up some spreadsheets, research on the internet, and discuss our plans with others. Expert advice, fact-checking, and case studies help. We can set aside a cash reserve and include flexibility and contingencies in our plan. We can consider the "what ifs" and draft "Plan B" and "Plan C."

STRENGTHEN

Prepare yourself
for what is to come.

We've taken a big step. Now is the time to fortify ourselves thoroughly and realistically for what is to come. We reinforce our boundaries. Muscle up for the work at hand. We grow a thicker skin, manage our time more efficiently, or simply work *smarter*—not harder.

The Universe is bringing it on! Get all your ducks in a row. Make sure to attend to legal and business matters now. Small details can make or break our endeavor. Timing is important. Examine the schedule and watch for double-bookings and over-commitment. We're going to need every ounce of strength for the work ahead.

Like the hunter who wrestles the forces of nature as well as enemies and beasts, we build resilience against all antagonistic forces. Take some time to focus on the target. Just as the hunter singles out one buffalo from the herd, so we hone in on and prepare for the specific outcome we seek. We invoke our goal *spiritually* before setting out. The radiance and power of our ambition strengthens us for this undertaking. Success is ours!

ARTWORK:

"Buffalo Medicine"

DEEPER INSIGHTS

The warrior strengthens himself for the battle to come.
The battle is finding food. He may have to wander far
and risk his life against warring tribes or a mighty beast.
His heart sings with the buffalo spirit. Power wells up as
he prepares to do what he must.

This **Fire** card features dynamic light that strengthens our spirit and guides our actions toward success. A **Crystal** magnifies the moonlight, representing the time cycles required for achievement.

The **Buffalo** or **Bull** symbolizes masculine strength, vitality, endurance, and protection. This sacred hero animal is our helper towards the goal. The buffalo's sacrifice creates our necessities of food, clothing, and shelter. Strengthening resembles a hunt—or a coming storm. We "batten the hatches," and shield ourselves in order to stay neutral and grounded when pitted against powerful forces.

The **Warrior's** strength comes from deep inside. A **Geode** symbolizes the resilient cluster of thoughts, tools, and experiences that drive him onward—the unbreakable gems of his strength.

REVERSED

We're resisting the true nature of our challenge. We minimize our opponents or over-estimate our ability to succeed. The tsunami is about to strike. A helpful friend can protect us now.

STUCK

Turn to others for help.
Then act on their advice.

Stuck is a hard place to be. Despite our best efforts, we're bogged down. We can't move forward and don't know how we got here. We can't lose the weight, climb the ladder, or make a relationship work. Our whole life feels stale. Beating ourselves up only sinks us lower in the swamp. Our self-talk is stagnant: *"Something's wrong with me." "I'm such a loser." "Everyone else is better."* The cycle of judgment leads to shame and exhaustion. Being stuck is like being trapped in a spiderweb. The web is our unconscious fear of rejection, of not deserving, or of ending up alone. We're lost and lonely in our "terminal uniqueness."

Fortunately, when we understand that we're just like others, we come unstuck! The stars might not favor us, and we might need extra self-love, patience, and determination, but we can get *moving* again. We try our best to be "teachable." One by one, we brush away webs of illusion. After we've spent all our anger, discouragement, and hopelessness on being stuck, we become willing to try something *different*. We ask others for help, hire a coach, join a recovery group, or get therapy.

We have faith in the Universe's deep goodness and become willing to truly listen to people's suggestions.

ARTWORK:

"Waiting For The Miracle"

ELEMENT: ▽ WATER   NUMBER: **1**   PHASE: **STASIS**

A young woman sits swamped in defeat. She's been there a long time, trapped in disappointment, self-pity, and negative thoughts. There's no energizing breeze. The web points in every direction to the way out, but in the end leads nowhere.

Stuck is the first **Water** card, before water starts moving. Here, the **Bubble** is water's skin of resistance that isolates us from the outside world. Our hidden animal helper is the **Spider** with her ability to slip and glide over the water's surface. Spider builds her **Web** in a neglected place—but fortunately, such a place is right beside a door, gate, or window that leads us out! Metaphysically, the spider helps us find the connection between worlds. Have you ever tried to catch a spider, only to have it disappear? In this way, the spider is our liaison from one situation to the next. The spiderweb represents the fragility of reality: the entangling veil of deception is actually our illusions about being "stuck," because the web also represents the fabric of creation and the possibility to weave a different situation from new perspectives and convictions.

REVERSED

Either we are in denial about our situation, or we don't yet realize we're stuck. Until we can feel the blockage, we believe we're making progress when the only "place" we get is exhausted! Other cards in our spread indicate what's going on, or we can pull a new card to hint the way out.

SURRENDER

Let the Universe
take command.

When progress is blocked and we've fought our best to advance, the only option left is to surrender. We finally accept our reality. Surrender is less about giving up than it is to simply *allow* and *admit* what is. When we stop forcing our will, things get surprisingly easier and obstacles dissolve in unexpected ways. The Universe takes care of the situation for us.

Our lessons are often challenging and painful while we are going through them. We can't understand the Great Mystery of how the Universe works, no matter how we try. Yet life tends to make sense in retrospect. Hardships turn out to be spiritual gifts. Our "enemies" end up being life's best teachers. Human weakness is our strength in disguise. Our goal is not to be "large and in charge," but instead to surrender our entire being and align with the Universe's mystical design. Fixing, figuring out, and manipulating are small, selfish attempts to bend life to our will. When we submit to our proper place in the scheme and let the Universe work on us and through us, a power greater than ourselves restores order, peace, and equilibrium.

"I Surrender"

*A beautiful young woman falls back and floats
in crystal pure water. She rests safely in the kind,
capable hands of a Higher Self.*

The **Water** in this card is calm, ideal for floating in submission. As the saying goes, we can't "push the river." We acquiesce and drift effortlessly in a state of relief. Surrender is the first movement of stagnant water, the release of pent-up emotions that had no place to go. We open our hearts and let ourselves be carried to unknown experiences.

The **Giant** hands symbolize an order of magnitude between the human and the Divine. Our highest self dwells in perfect alignment with the Universe. We surrender to this aspect of our being, aware of how small and powerless we are to affect forces beyond our control.

REVERSED

Our ego resists surrender. It's hard to admit defeat and accept powerlessness. We still think we can figure it out or control destiny by brute force. **Fire** and **Air** cards show us the work to be done. Look to the spread or pull another card for inspiration.

TEMPTATION

Investigate before risking
 your money . . . or your heart.

If it sounds too good to be true, it probably is. Optimism mixed with daydreams leads to "magical thinking" and promises of a rose-colored world. We yearn for happier times, more love, greater comfort, and extra prosperity. No wonder we fall prey to temptation! Everywhere, advertisements promise us instant weight loss, the secret of youth, or a "perfect match." We hope to win the lottery, be rescued by the knight in shining armor, or land our dream job, only to get deceived. Desperation and impatience only hijack us into false beliefs and compulsive choices.

Temptation is a warning to slow down before committing. We take care before answering, "Yes!" We scrutinize new acquaintances and involvements prior to signing. Poke around, do more research, or let some time pass before takeoff. Jekyll-and-Hyde types soon betray themselves. Scammers and cheats expose their greed to those who resist. Open the drawers and look under the rug. Ask lots of hard questions or take a trial run before "getting into bed."

It's tempting to rush into romance and "quick" riches. When we slow down, we find that things may not be what they seem . . .

ARTWORK:

"Step Right Up"

DEEPER INSIGHTS

An enchantress beckons us into a rosy pink world.
Her smile is bewitching. We can't wait to enter!
Rides and amusements float on cotton-candy clouds.
If only we could take a break from the daily drudge,
or go back to being a carefree little kid again. But if we
enter the illusion, we soon find ourselves abandoned,
broke, and scammed out of our self-esteem.

This **Air** card reveals through a veil an illusory world that seems real enough. A **Carnival** floats on cotton-candy clouds, tempting us to lose ourselves in pleasures of fun and excitement. Temptation heightens the difference between *acting* and *reacting*. A limited-time offer tempts us to react. But reaction is a reflex, not a conscious choice. Pressure hurries us to grab the treasure before it's gone. By taking time to check in with our deeper feelings, the experience of friends, or by calling on our Spirit Guides, we avoid deception and waste. We forfeit a quick "prize" but win the lasting glory of intact self-respect.

REVERSED

We're unaware of the danger and unwilling to believe its there. We may have to go ahead and get the full lesson the hard way. Again. Or, ask the cards for guidance on how to resist the irresistible and instead make a balanced decision.

TRICKSTER

Laugh at your "mistakes"

then start again.

The Trickster has deceived us . . . again! Just when we thought things were getting better, it all falls to ruins. Again. And is that Clown, that old Fool, actually *laughing* at us?! What does it take for us to get the joke—and finally laugh at ourselves?!

We take life so seriously sometimes. The Trickster reminds us to see the funny side of human being. We can have a good cry, but make sure to follow it with an equally good belly laugh. Our so-called "mistakes" are nothing less than experiments in the endless cosmic play. Lightness and laughter cure our "failures" by reminding us we're not in control.

As the saying goes, "Wherever I go, there I am." We may be tempted to try a "geographical cure," and move away from problems. But we can't get away from ourselves, for better or worse. Our problems and patterns travel with us. Change begins and ends in ourselves as an "inside job," whose most essential ingredient we often leave out: a sense of humor!

ARTWORK:

"Wherever I Go, There I Am"

ELEMENT: △ AIR   NUMBER: **1**   PHASE: **BEGINNING**

DEEPER INSIGHTS

The Jester leaps above the clouds, juggling the Platonic solids along with the sphere that represents totality.

The first **Air** card shows the **Trickster** above the clouds with both feet off the ground. The Joker is the only one who can risk telling the truth to the king. Since he is a fool, there's nothing to lose because who takes him seriously? Yet the Trickster is really the sage, metaphysically speaking. His **Mask** hides the truth behind playful foolery.

The sacred geometry known as the **Platonic Solids** were believed to be the fundamental building blocks of all matter in the Universe. They remind us that we have everything we need, no matter what phase we're in:

Tetrahedron · Fire   Cube · Earth
Octahedron · Air   Icosahedron · Water
Dodecahedron · God   Gold · Creative Principle

Behind the Trickster is the **Seed of Life**, the emblem of renewal. When things go "wrong," we can always return to the fundamental laws at the nucleus of all endeavors.

REVERSED

We still think we're in control, on top of the situation. We get that it's back to basics, but we aren't laughing. It's time to go toss a ball for some fun and lightness. What goes up must come down, and just might bounce! Physical play opens us up. For fun, pull another card. It might just bring us back down to **Earth**!

WISDOM

Take command of You!
Give yourself permission.

There comes a time when we simply *know* what we *know.* We no longer second-guess ourselves or ask others what they think. We listen to our gut, our experience, and our hard-won wisdom about life. Then we take action, knowing we can be confident in ourselves.

Too often we give away our power, thinking others have more expertise, or we are somehow inferior. Yet if we don't value ourselves, who will? Life is a constant power struggle. From the moment we're born, people boss us around, give us orders, and try to control us. We need to take back our power, rule our time and decisions, and say, "No!" when we mean no. Our ideas and aspirations may sound "crazy" to others, but they are *ours* to try, as we see fit. No one can live our lives for us.

In all Creation, there's only one of us! Let ourselves know what we know. Forget about what others think. Be true to ourself, and *be* our True Self. Release old insecurities. Accept the things we can't change about life, then get to work on the things in our command. Embrace and accept *maturity.* Continuing to put other people's opinions and ideas in front of our own only leads to disappointment, regret, and frustration. If necessary, write out a script and practice what we need to say, so we're ready when confronted. Raise the flaming sword of truth like the Queen. Affirm, "I have the right to speak for myself!"

DEEPER INSIGHTS

A Queen sits on her horse. She holds the sword of truth to the skies, clearing all negative karma. The heavens open in response and she is empowered.

The second-last **Air** card takes us to the apex before our return to **Earth**. Our Queen holds the **Flaming Sword of Truth**. Metaphysically, this sword cuts away ignorance and evil from others. Imagine slashing a hole in the darkness to reveal Divine Light behind! The truth of the Universe supports our unique individual tendencies and ideas. We are valid, witnessed, powerful at last.

The **Unicorn**, our curiously unique mythical animal helper, is a celestial creature of heaven, rainbows, and the sun. He transports us through mists of insecurity to the realm of self-mastery, majesty, and ascension. The **Northern Lights** are Earth's portal to cosmic powers and mysteries. Our Unicorn carries us to the highest wisdom.

REVERSED

We're still too concerned about what others think. We stay silent and agreeable instead of speaking out. The key to standing our ground comes from our hearts in self-love. If we fear loss because of speaking our truth, is that situation really in our highest interests? Look for **Water** cards to see how to stop accepting the unacceptable and set some boundaries.

CONNECT ONLINE

Discover additional interpretations and meanings for each card online at:

transformation-oracle.com

For *Transformation Oracle* classes with Sonya, or to find out how you can become a Certified Reader of this deck, please visit:

transformation-oracle.com/certification

JOIN OUR

TRANSFORMATION ORACLE

FACEBOOK GROUP

If you're on Facebook, you're invited to join this special group. It's a safe place to:

- Share spreads, including your thoughts & questions
- Add insights and interpretations to help others

Login to Facebook, then go to our group at:

www.facebook.com/groups/TransformationOracle

To follow Sonya, please LIKE her page at:

www.facebook.com/SonyaShannonArtist

TRANSFORMATION ORACLE CARDS BY ELEMENT

This table helps you explore stages of self-development using the 4 elements. Each element progresses through 11 transformations. For celestial guidance, locate cards from your reading below to chart your soul's journey.

▽ EARTH	△ AIR	△ FIRE	▽ WATER
1 Journey	1 Trickster	1 Renovation	1 Stuck
2 Descent	2 Direction	2 Purification	2 Surrender
3 Discovery	3 Receptivity	3 Liberation	3 Prayer
4 Contemplation	4 Temptation	4 Reflection	4 Initiation
5 Rest	5 Knowledge	5 Perspective	5 Innocence
6 Simplicity	6 Strategy	6 Strengthen	6 Intuition
7 Recycle	7 Immigration	7 Quickening	7 Resurrection
8 Harvest	8 Integration	8 Grace	8 Expansion
9 Forgiveness	9 Ascent	9 Emergence	9 Connection
10 Generosity	10 Wisdom	10 Creativity	10 Resolution
11 Separation	11 Reversal	11 Rebirth	11 Celebration

ACKNOWLEDGMENTS

The *Transformation Oracle* cards and guidebook would not have been possible without the love, encouragement, and support of many people, to whom I am more grateful than words can express.

The suggestion to make healing cards came from Maureen "Mo" Bacon, whose insights, wisdom, and cheer are woven throughout this product. My "doula" Karen Blair found models, organized and helped with photo shoots, advised on business aspects, and encouraged me endlessly. My soulmate and husband Tim Binkley brought his artistry, kindness, and support to every decision large and small. Without him, I would in no measure be the artist and author I have become. Janis "Rooby" Page provided wonderful critiques of both artwork and writing, and expanded my understanding of organizational wisdoms like the four elements. Kathleen Kennedy provided much-welcomed donations, praise, and encouragement. My niece Sarah helped with photo shoots and lent her experience as an exhibiting artist. Kristina Eisenhower encouraged me in every way, all the way from Japan! Heartfelt thanks to my dear family, Laura and Canute Haferkorn, Krista and Lakis Christou, Lisa and Ross McLeod, Stasia and Steve Andersen, Shelley Binkley, and the Baker, Tatem and Binkley families, without whose continuous cheerleading, praise, support, and advice this project would never exist. A very special thanks to all the dancers, actors, models, moms, and dads who helped with costumes, locations, and animals. Deepest thanks to my students and fans, and to Pete Schiffer, Chris McClure, my editor Dinah Roseberry, and everyone at Schiffer Books for your endless help. God bless you all!

SONYA SHANNON

SONYA SHANNON has had a successful career as a digital effects artist and educator that spans Canada, the USA, and Asia. She graduated from the prestigious classical animation program at Sheridan College and taught computer art and 3-D computer animation in the MFA programs at School of Visual Arts and Pratt Institute in New York City. Her distinctive style is shaped by her training in hand-drawn animation, expertise in digital color, and work on the frontier of special effects.

Highlights of her career include effects on *Star Trek III: The Search for Spock,* a stint as a creative director at Broadway Video (home of *Saturday Night Live*), and a pioneer digital version of Josef Albers' "Interaction of Color," shown at the Guggenheim Museum in New York.

Her long-time work as an I-Ching reader led Sonya to create the *Transformation Oracle*. As a spiritual healer, Sonya has worked with survivors of childhood abuse and serves as a ULC Minister. She has published articles on computer animation and digital art, as well as select poems. Sonya is currently working on a graphic novel.

Browse Sonya's art portfolio at **artware.com.** Read Sonya's blog at **sonya-shannon.com.**

DISCLAIMER: The author's intent is to provide general suggestions to help guide you on your spiritual journey. In the event you use any of the information in this book as part of your healing process, the author assumes no responsibility for your actions.